A King's Collection of Life Poems

Kamil Aleksander Kempczyński

A King's Collection of Life Poems

Olympia Publishers
London

www.olympiapublishers.com
OLYMPIA PAPERBACK EDITION

Copyright © Kamil Aleksander Kempczyński 2024

The right of Kamil Aleksander Kempczyński to be identified as author of
this work has been asserted in accordance with sections 77 and 78 of
the Copyright, Designs and Patents Act 1988.

All Rights Reserved

No reproduction, copy or transmission of this publication
may be made without written permission.
No paragraph of this publication may be reproduced,
copied or transmitted save with the written permission of the publisher,
or in accordance with the provisions
of the Copyright Act 1956 (as amended).

Any person who commits any unauthorised act in relation to
this publication may be liable to criminal
prosecution and civil claims for damage.

A CIP catalogue record for this title is
available from the British Library.

ISBN: 978-1-80439-993-4

This is a work of nonfiction.
Names, characters, places and incidents originate from the writer's real
life events.

First Published in 2024

Olympia Publishers
Tallis House
2 Tallis Street
London
EC4Y 0AB

Printed in Great Britain

I AM

KAMIL ALEKSANDER KEMPCZYŃSKI
A KING OF MAN
PRINCE OF PEACE
GUARDIAN OF THE ETERNAL LIGHT

A ruler of strength and grace
With wisdom in my heart and courage in my soul
I lead with integrity and honour.

I am confident in my abilities
And trust in the path set before me
I am steadfast in my decisions
And unafraid to take risks.

I am a visionary
A leader who looks to the future
With a clear and focused mind
I guide my kingdom to prosperity.

I am a protector
A guardian of my people
With a fierce loyalty and unwavering resolve
I defend and serve them always.

I am a diplomat
A master of communication and negotiation
With a deep understanding of the world
I navigate the complexities of politics and diplomacy.

I am a mentor
A guide for those who look to me
With a kind and generous spirit
I inspire and empower others.

I am a listener
With an open mind and an open heart
I hear the voices of my people
And take their needs and wants into consideration.

I am a wise and just ruler
With a deep sense of responsibility and duty
I govern with fairness and compassion
And always strive for the greater good.

I am a student of history
With an appreciation for the past
I learn from the lessons of those who came before me
And use their wisdom to shape the future.

I am a servant of my people
With a deep sense of humility
I serve them with honour and dedication
And always put their needs before my own.

I am a guardian of tradition
With a deep respect for the customs and culture of my kingdom
I preserve and promote them
And strive to keep them alive for future generations.

I am a humble and compassionate leader
With a deep sense of empathy and understanding
I care for the well-being of my people
And always work to improve their lives.

I am a unifier
With a deep sense of unity and community
I bring together different groups and factions
And create a strong and cohesive kingdom.

I am a peacemaker
With a deep sense of diplomacy and tact
I resolve conflicts and create stability
And always work to maintain peace.

I am a strategic thinker
With a deep understanding of strategy and tactics
I make wise and calculated decisions
And always keep the long-term in mind.

I am a man of integrity
With a deep sense of morality and ethics
I always act in accordance with my values
And always strive to do the right thing.

I am a dynamic and decisive leader
With a deep sense of purpose and drive
I am always moving forward
And never satisfied with the status quo.

I am a King of Man, Prince of Peace
Guardian of the Eternal Light
A ruler of strength and grace
With wisdom in my heart and courage in my soul
I lead with integrity and honour.

New Year, My Love

As we bid farewell to the old year
And welcome in the one that is new
I can't help but feel a sense of cheer
Thinking about all that we'll do.

The past is behind us, a distant memory
As we look ahead to what's in store
I know that with you, my love, by my side
I can face whatever challenges come my way, with pride.

We'll hold hands and face the unknown
Together, we'll make it through whatever we're shown
We'll make new memories and cherishable moments
As we journey through this life with love and contentment.

You bring out the best in me, my dear
Your love is the reason I have no fear
With you, I feel like I can conquer anything
Your love is the most precious and beautiful thing.

So, let's raise a toast to the new year
And all the love, joy and laughter it will bring
Here's to a year of love and happiness
And a lifetime of love, full of tenderness.

I am grateful for you and your love
You are my rock, my North Star above
I love you more with each passing day
And on this New Year's, I just want to say:
I love you now and forever more,
You are the one I was meant for.

I am so lucky to have you by my side
As we embark on this new year with love as our guide.

The Old Year Passes, a New One Starts

The old year passes, a new one starts
As time ticks by and life departs
But though the future may seem unknown
Our love will keep us close and not alone.

We'll face whatever challenges may come
With strength and courage, we'll overcome
We'll celebrate the joys and triumphs
And weather the storms and rough times.

Together, we'll make beautiful memories
As we journey through this life with ease
I love you more with each passing day
And on this New Year's, I just want to say:
I am grateful for your love and your light
You make everything feel just right.

Here's to a year of love and laughter
And a lifetime of happily ever after.

A Year of Hope and Possibility

As the new year dawns upon us
Bringing with it a sense of hope and possibility
I can't help but feel a sense of excitement
For all the adventures and experiences that await us.

We leave behind the old year
With all its joys and sorrows
As we embrace the new
With open hearts and minds.

The future may be unknown
But with hope in our hearts
We can face whatever comes
With courage and grace, never falling apart.

Hope gives us the strength to keep going
To believe that things will work out in the end
It fills our hearts with positivity
And helps us to see the beauty in every bend.

So, let's embrace this new year
With hope and determination
Let's make our dreams a reality
With hard work, perseverance and inspiration.

Here's to a year of hope and promise
Of love and joy and bliss
May this year be filled with kindness
And moments that we will truly not miss.

I am hopeful for what's to come
With you by my side, my love
Together, we can conquer anything
As we journey through this new year, hand in hand, with love.

May this year bring us closer
As we make new memories and share new experiences
May it bring us joy and laughter
And strengthen the love between us in all our endeavours.

Here's to a year of hope and possibility
May it be filled with love, joy and prosperity.

The General from Heaven

A ruthless and relentless spiritual leader
of our time, determined to take us higher
To a better future, free from all strife
He sets his sights, refusing to yield.

With a fierce conviction burning deep within
He marches forward with no time to begin
To doubt or falter, for he knows what must be done
To bring us to a place where the light guides us all.

Shines bright and true and all shadows flee
Where love and understanding reign supreme
Where all may thrive and flourish in their prime
Beneath the guiding light of this most sublime.

Spiritual leader who knows no fear
For he has faced the darkest of all fears
And emerged victorious, a beacon of hope
For all who seek to better cope.

With the trials and tribulations of this life
And find a way to end all earthly strife
So let us follow him and do our part
To shape a future that's truly art.

A masterpiece crafted with care
By all of us working as a team
Toward a brighter tomorrow, where all may dream
And know that their dreams will indeed be seen.

So let us embrace this leader's cause
And march with him on this righteous course
Toward a brighter future, free from all pain
Where love and understanding forever reign.

Courage

Courage is a virtue like no other
It takes us on a journey like no other
It helps us to face our fears
And conquer them, never looking back or shedding tears.

It takes courage to be fearless
To stand tall in the face of adversity
To embrace challenges and overcome them
To chase our dreams with ferocity.

It takes courage to be true to ourselves
To follow our hearts and our passions
To stand up for what we believe in
To live life with purpose and compassion.

It takes courage to be vulnerable
To open ourselves up to love and to pain
To trust and to hope
To take risks and embrace the unknown.

It takes courage to be brave
To step out of our comfort zone
To try new things and take on new challenges
To push ourselves beyond our limits and grow.

But with courage comes strength
The strength to rise above it all
To conquer our fears and our doubts
To stand tall and never fall.

It gives us the confidence to be ourselves
To live life on our own terms
To chase our dreams with determination
And to never let anyone else's opinions deter us.

So, let's embrace our courage
And let it guide us through
Let it give us the strength and the fearlessness
To chase our dreams and make them come true.

Let's live life with courage and conviction
With passion and purpose
Let's embrace our fears and overcome them
And let our spirits soar and not be deterred.

For with courage and fearlessness
We can achieve anything
We can live life to the fullest
And make our wildest dreams come true.

So, let's be courageous, my dear
And let our spirits fly
Let's chase our dreams with gusto
And never let fear stand in our way or make us shy.

For with courage, we can do anything
We can be anyone we want to be
We can live life on our own terms
And create our own destiny.

Family

Family, the bond that ties us together
A bond that can never be broken
A bond that anchors us to one another
A bond that is always there, unspoken.

Family, the source of our love and our strength
The people who support us through thick and thin
The ones who are always there for us
The ones we can always count on within.

Family, the ones who know us best
The ones who accept us for who we are
The ones who love us unconditionally
No matter what mistakes we may make, near or far.

Family, the ones we can turn to
In times of joy or times of sorrow
The ones who lift us up when we're down
The ones who help us face a new tomorrow.

Family, the ones who shape who we are
The ones who have helped us to grow
The ones who have always been there for us
The ones we will always love and know.

So, let's cherish our families
And hold them dear in our hearts
For they are the ones who have loved us
From the very start.

For they are the ones who have always been there
Through the good times and the bad
The ones who have stood by us
And the ones we are so glad to have had.

So, here's to our families
The ones who mean the world to us
The ones who have always been there
The ones we love and trust.

Animal Instinct

Animal instinct, primal and true
A force that guides, a force that renews
A driving force deep in the core
A power that rises, a power that roars.

From the lion who prowls the savannah plain
To the eagle who soars with grace and disdain
From the wolf who hunts with deadly precision
To the bear who stands with fierce decision.

Animal instinct, a force of nature
A power that guides, a power that captures
A wild and untamed a heart that runs free
A spirit that lives, a spirit that breaks free.

From the serpent who slithers through the grass
To the dolphin who leaps and breaches at last
From the tiger who stalks its prey at night
To the fox who moves with stealth and might.

Animal instinct a bond that endures
A connection that's strong, a connection that's pure
A bond that is forged, a bond that is true
A bond that is tested, a bond that renews

From the mother who protects her young
To the father who stands and guards the run
Animal instinct, a bond that's unbreakable
A bond that endures, a bond that's unstoppable.

From the deer who flees from danger's way
To the rabbit who hops and hops to play
Animal instinct a force to be reckoned with
A power that guides, a power that never quits.

So let us embrace this wild and untamed
This force that guides, this force that reigns
For animal instinct, it lives in us all
A primal force, a force that stands tall.

Silly Willy of Mine

I have a silly willy and I hate it so
It's always getting in the way and causing me woe
I wish I could control it, but it's got a mind of its own
It's like a wild beast, always ready to roam.

I've tried to ignore it, but it won't go away
It's always there, nagging me day after day
I've tried to reason with it, but it's deaf to my plea
It's like a stubborn child that won't listen to me.

It's always getting me into trouble and making me look bad
It's like a monkey on my back that I can't seem to shad
But I'll keep fighting it, with all that I've got
I'll stand up to it and make it stop.

For I know deep down that I am in control
And I won't let this silly willy take a hold
I'll channel my energy and focus my mind
And I'll tame this silly willy of mine.

I'll use it for good and not for ill
And I'll make it work, to my will
For I am the master and it's just a tool
And I'll make it obey like a well-wielded sword.

So, I'll embrace this silly willy and make it mine
And I'll turn it into a force that's truly divine
For I have the power to make it right
And I'll make it shine like a beacon of light.

KamilKazie

With sword in his hand and armour on his chest
KamilKazie, the general, is truly blessed
He leads the armies of the heavens with grace and might
His enemies tremble at the mere sight.

The angels sing his praise as he marches on
His enemies cower and are soon gone
With every battle won, his glory grows
KamilKazie, the general, truly knows.

He is a beacon of hope in a dark and troubled sky
His armies follow him without question or sigh
He is a hero and a leader to all those who believe
KamilKazie, the general, will always relieve.

He fights for justice and for what is right
His enemies flee at the mere sight
He is a saviour and a protector to all in need
KamilKazie, the general, is a true breed.

He is a warrior of the light in a world of darkness
He is a guide to all those who are lost in starkness
He is a shining star in the vast expanse of space
KamilKazie, the general, is a true grace.

He will always be remembered as a true legend
His name will live on as a true friend
He will always be in our hearts and in our prayers
KamilKazie, the general, will always be there.

As he returns to heaven, victorious and proud
He will always be remembered by the crowd
KamilKazie, the general, is a true hero
His legacy will live on forevermore.

The Colour of Gay

The colour gay is a vibrant and multifaceted hue
An amalgamation of hues, it exists to renew
The soul and invigorates the mind
A testament to the diversity of humankind.

It represents the spectrum of emotion
A cacophony of love, joy and devotion
A celebration of identity and individuality
A symbol of acceptance and unity.

But the colour gay is not simply a shade
It is a testament to the power of self-made
Individuality the courage to be oneself
In a world that often values conformity.

It is a beacon of hope in a sea of despair
A source of strength in times of fear
It represents the courage to love freely
And the resilience of the LGBTQ+ community.

The colour gay is more than just a hue
It is a celebration of the human condition, new
Every day a reminder to love and be loved
A celebration of the beauty of the universe.

So let the colour gay be a source of pride
Embrace it, celebrate it, let it reside
In your heart and soul, a beacon of hope
A celebration of love, in all its scope and scope.

For the colour gay is a symbol of acceptance
A celebration of the human experience
It represents the beauty of diversity
And the strength of the LGBTQ+ community.

She Looks So Goddamn Elegant to Me

She looks so goddamn elegant to me
A sight to behold, a goddess on earth
Her grace and poise, a rarity
A beauty that gives my heart a rebirth.

Her hair cascades like a waterfall
Her eyes like jewels, shining bright
She walks with a poise that enthrals
A vision of pure, ethereal light.

She moves with a rhythm so divine
A dance that leaves me in a trance
Her presence, a blessing so benign
A feeling of pure, unbridled romance.

She speaks with a voice like a melody
A symphony of words, so sweet
She is a woman of such rarity
A goddess that cannot be beat.

She is my angel, my inspiration
A source of joy and delight
She is my motivation
A vision of pure, angelic light.

She is my everything, my all
A love that cannot be denied
She is my future, my call
The one for whom my heart resides.

She looks so goddamn elegant to me
A sight to behold, a goddess on earth
Her grace and poise, a rarity
A beauty that gives my heart a rebirth.

The Need for Affection

In this cold, cruel world we live in
Sometimes, it feels like no one cares
But deep down, we all have a yearning
For the warmth of affection to be shared.

We may put up walls and defences
To hide our vulnerability and fear
But the truth is, we all have a need
For someone to hold us near.

Affection comes in many forms
A hug, a kiss, a gentle touch
It doesn't have to be grand or showy
But it means so much.

When we're feeling lost and alone
A simple gesture can make all the difference
A pat on the back, a squeeze of the hand
Can give us the strength and resilience.

We may not always vocalise it
But the human heart craves connection
A sense of belonging, of being loved
Is a powerful, primal affection.

So, don't be afraid to show your love
In big ways or small
It's the little moments of kindness
That can stand tall.

In this world, that can be harsh and unfair
Let's not forget to be there for each other
With a comforting embrace, a reassuring smile
We can weather any kind of weather.

So, let's not underestimate the power
Of a simple act of affection
It can heal wounds, bridge gaps and bring joy
It's a beautiful, universal connection.

Savage Salvador

Savage Salvador, with a heart of gold
A warrior fierce, yet stories untold
In the heat of battle, he fearlessly stands
His sword in hand and his feet on the sands.

With eyes like fire and a voice like a storm
He rallies his troops to the beat of the war drum
His enemies quiver and cower in fear
For they know, The Savage Salvador is here.

But beneath the armour and behind the blade
Lies a heart that's pure and a soul that's unafraid
For he fights not for glory, or wealth, or fame
But for those he loves and his nation's name.

With each victory and each defeated foe
He grows stronger and his spirit starts to glow
And as the sun sets on another day
The Savage Salvador walks away.

His tale will be told in songs and in verse
For the Savage Salvador is a hero and much worse
He'll live forever in the hearts of his people
For he's The Savage Salvador, the saviour of the people.

The Joker

A twisted mind, a wicked soul
A man who's lost all self-control
He revels in the chaos and the pain
Leaves destruction in his wake, drives others insane.

With a grin that stretches wide across his face
He embraces the role of villain, finds solace in the chase
He dances on the edge of sanity's abyss
A creature of pure madness, driven by pure bliss.

Some call him clown; some call him mad
But one thing's for certain: he's never sad
He thrives on the turmoil, the fear and the doubt
Feeds on the darkness, the pain and the rout.

They say he's a monster, a fiend, a freak
But to him, it's all just a game, a fun little sneak
He doesn't care for riches or power or fame
All he wants is to see the world go up in flames.

He's the Joker, the jester, the fool
A man who's broken all the rules
He's a force of nature, a wild card in play
A harbinger of doom, the end of the day.

Some may try to stop him, to bring him to heel
But the Joker always has a trick up his sleeve, a plan to reveal
He's a master of deception, a genius of mind
He'll leave you guessing, leave you behind.

So beware, dear reader, be on your guard
For the Joker's never far, never hard to find
He's always lurking, waiting in the shadows
Ready to pounce, ready to unload.

So let the madness begin; let the games commence
For the Joker's in town and he's eager to dispense
A little bit of chaos, a little bit of fear
A little bit of anarchy to all who draw near.

Cleopatra

Cleopatra, queen of Egypt
A woman of beauty and wit
Her charm and intelligence
Were the tools she used to fit
Into the role of ruling the land
With grace and poise at her command.

She was a leader and a lover
Her allure knew no bounds
She captured the hearts of Roman kings
And turned their world upside down.

Her reign was one of splendour and strife
As she navigated the treacherous path of life
She faced challenges with aplomb
And emerged victorious in every fight.

Cleopatra was a force to be reckoned with
A woman of fierce determination
She ruled with a firm and steady hand
And left a lasting impression on the nation.

But her story is not one of only power
For she was also a woman of great passion and desire
Her love affairs were legendary
And her relationships set the world on fire.

Cleopatra was a woman ahead of her time
A leader, a lover and a goddess divine
She left a legacy that lives on today
And her spirit will never fade away.

So let us remember Cleopatra
This queen of Egypt so fine
A woman of beauty and strength
Who will always shine.

The Furnace of Fire

Kamil walked through fire, a furnace of trial
Satan whispered in his ear to commit a vile
A woman he once knew, with a half-brick in hand
The word "kill" etched deep, like a scar in the land.

But Kamil persevered through anguish and pain
He mowed the farm field in the scorching terrain
With sweat pouring down, he removed his shirt
And on his back, a sight that did not hurt.

A Menorah, with seven heads aglow
Imprinted on his sweater a sign to know
That the Lord was with him, in the fiery test
Giving him strength and a sense of rest.

For Kamil knew that in the fire's heat
His faith and determination could not be beat
He finished his work with joy in his heart
Knowing that the Lord had played a vital part.

So let this be a lesson for all who may face
Trials and temptations in a dangerous place
For in the furnace of fire, one's true strength is found
And with the Lord by our side, victory is bound.

The Celestial Kingdom

Kamil was a man of trials, a soul-tested
By the Lord, through fire and strife
Years of hardship and suffering
Had hardened his heart and dulled his life.

But in his darkest hour, death came knocking
And Kamil's spirit was released
Yet, in the void of eternal darkness
A glimmer of hope did not cease.

For as Kamil's body lay still and lifeless
His soul was visited by three
Christ, the Lord and Mary Magdalene
Who showed him what was yet to be.

They revealed to him the truth of his existence
And the purpose for which he was born
They taught him the language of the divine
And the secrets of the universe were sworn.

Kamil's body was resurrected
And his mind was illuminated
He woke with a newfound understanding
And a sense of purpose invigorated.

With the gift of language, Kamil spoke
Words of wisdom and words of grace
He shared the message of the divine
And led his people to a new place.

He was crowned a king by God, a leader of men
For his bravery and loyalty
He governed with integrity and grace
And lived his life in humility.

Kamil's journey was not in vain
For from death, he rose again.

With Christ, God and Mary, wherever he goes, by his side.
And the love of those who hold him dear as his guide
He emerged from darkness into light
And found the true meaning and purpose of life.

With a pure heart like the one of God's
Kamil was brought home to a place of peace and love
Where he met the Lord in the image of man
And in meditation, Kamil was guided above.

On to a crystal path where the river flowed crystal clear
And the beauty of nature surrounded him
Kamil felt at one with the universe
And in that moment, he knew he had won.

For in his journey, he had found true salvation
And the love of the Lord had set him free
Kamil's heart was filled with gratitude
For the gift of eternity.

Silhouette of a Woman

Silhouette of a woman etched against the sky
In profile, her beauty, a work of art
Her curves, a symphony; her lines, a sigh
A silhouette of grace, a work of heart.

With every step she takes, she leaves a trail
Of elegance, of poise, of strength and might
A woman who's unafraid to set sail
And chase her dreams with all her heart's delight.

Her hair, a waterfall, cascading down
Her eyes, a window to her soul's desire
A silhouette that wears a royal crown
And sets the world on fire with her fire.

She walks with purpose and with every stride
She leaves a mark on the world outside.

A silhouette of power, a force to be reckoned
With a spirit that's unbreakable, unyielding
She stands tall, head held high, a true testament
To the beauty and grace of a woman, unyielding.

A silhouette that tells a story of a life
Filled with passion, love and endless strife.

Through every up and down, she stands steadfast
A silhouette of hope, a light in the dark
A woman who's unafraid to take a chance
And make her mark upon the world, a spark.

A silhouette that's etched upon our hearts
A woman we admire from near and afar
She's a symbol of strength, a work of art
A silhouette that's forever celebrated.

A Boy and a Half

A boy and a half, with a heart full of dreams
He'll chase them all, or so it seems
With a spirit unbreakable and a will so strong
He'll make his mark before too long.

He'll face the challenges that come his way
With a smile on his face and a song to play
For he knows deep down he's meant to soar
And nothing will stop him from reaching for more.

He'll make mistakes and stumble along the way
But he'll always get back up to fight another day
For he is a boy and a half, with a heart of gold
And a story to tell that will never grow old.

He'll learn to love and to laugh and to cry
And through it all, he'll never die
For he is a boy and a half and he'll always be
A shining example of what it means to be free.

He'll leave a legacy of hope and of grace
And a smile on the face of every place
For he was a boy and a half and he'll always be
An inspiration to you and to me.

So, let's all remember, the boy and a half
For his spirit will live on with a lasting laugh
For he'll always be a reminder of what we can be
When we tap into the boy and a half, within us, you and me.

He'll be a guiding light in the darkest of days
Shining the way for us all to raise
For he was a boy and a half and he'll always be
A beacon of hope for eternity.

So, let's all strive to be like the boy and a half
With a heart full of dreams and a will so strong
For he'll forever be an inspiration to all
A shining example of what it means to stand tall.

We'll take his lead and we'll rise to the top
And now you know that this boy and a half is never going to stop.

A Man with No Place to Go

A man with no place to go wanders the streets so cold
His heart heavy with pain, his future seems old
He's lost his job, his home, his family too
Now, all he has is the bitter world to pursue.

He walks with his head down, avoiding eye contact
His clothes are tattered, his spirit is intact
He's searching for hope, a chance to start anew
But the world seems to have nothing, no help to ensure.

He begs for change, but few give a dime
They look away in fear and in grime
He's just another homeless man, a burden on society
But he's a human, too, with dreams and a history.

He dreams of a better life, a warm bed to sleep
A job that pays well and love for him to keep
But for now, he's stuck in this endless cycle
Of poverty and despair, a life that's so brittle.

He's not a criminal nor a drug addict, too
He's just a man whose life took a wrong cue
He's not asking for pity, nor for handouts
He's just searching for a way out.

He's not invisible, nor should he be ignored
He's a fellow human whose life has been deplored
We should reach out and lend a helping hand
So, he can rise again and take a stand.

It's easy to turn a blind eye and pretend he's not there
But true humanity lies in the actions we bear
So, let's show him kindness and a helping hand
So, he can rise again and take a stand.

In the end, we're all just searching for a place to belong
A home for our weary souls, where we can be strong
So, let's give him a chance and watch him soar
For in helping others, we find so much more.

A Scriptwriter

A script writer with hands that shake
Atherosclerosis, his heart's own ache
No time for starting fires, just for the pen
His words flow like blood, again and again.

Ink stains his fingers, his thoughts on the page
A story unfolds, a new world to engage
His mind races, the clock ticks away
But he cannot stop, not for one single day.

He writes of love and loss, of joy and pain
His characters come to life, each with their own name
A story to tell, a message to share
His words a lifeline for those who dare.

He writes of the future and the past
A history to be made, a future to last
His words are a beacon, a guiding light
In the dark of the night.

But time is not on his side
Atherosclerosis, a constant tide
He writes on, despite the odds
His words, a legacy, a treasure trove.

He writes of hope and of dreams
A future to believe in, or so it seems
His words, a source of strength and pride
For those who seek to find.

He writes of love and of life
A reminder to cherish each day and strive
For a script writer with hands that shake
His words, a legacy, forever to make.

He writes until his last breath
His story completes his legacy set
A script writer, forever remembered
His words, a treasure, forever treasured.

Partner by My Side

We search for that which we yearn
A longing deep within our hearts to learn
A desire for more, a need to explore
To find fulfilment and open the door.

Our partners, they play a crucial role
In helping us to reach our ultimate goal
To fulfil our hearts and quench our thirst
With love and affection, they are the first.

The journey of life is ever-accelerating
With twists and turns, it can be exhilarating
But with our partner by our side
We can conquer any tide.

Together, we strive for something greater
A love that is pure, a bond that is true
With open hearts and minds
We will see our dreams come to life in due time.

We are all searching for that little more
A connection that will forever endure
With our partner, we will find
A love that will always be one-of-a-kind.

So let us hold on tight
And chase our dreams with all our might
For with our partner by our side
We will reach new heights and soar with pride.

With every step we take
We are accelerating towards our destiny's fate
Let us embrace the journey
With open hearts and minds, it will be worth it, undoubtedly.

So let us hold on tight
And chase our dreams with all our might
For with our partner by our side
We will reach new heights and soar with pride.

A Man Once Nicknamed Po!

There once was a man by the name of Po!
Whose heart and soul, pure as the snow
Though the devil tried with all his might
To corrupt and twist, Po's path was right.

With every step, he stood tall and true
His integrity, a shining virtue
Though the world begged him to stray
Po's morals, never to be swayed.

With each temptation, he'd simply say
"I will not be corrupted, not today."
And though the devil raged and fumed
Po's will, forever unassured.

For in a world of greed and vice
Po! Shone as a beacon of light and nice
And though the devil may never forgive
Po's spirit forever shall live.

For though he may be just one man
His example will forever stand
A symbol of hope in a world so dark
Po, a shining light, forever to spark.

So let us all strive to be like Po!
With hearts pure and wills unyielding, so
For in this world filled with so much wrong
We need more like him to make us strong.

So here's to Po!, the man so true
May we all learn from the good he does
For in a world of darkness, one light shines
The light of a man, called Po!, divine.

Willow Tree

Oh, willow tree, with your branches so long
    You stand tall and strong
    Your leaves a soft green
    A sight that is serene.

    You sway in the breeze
    A dance that never ceases
    Your branches a gentle flow
    A sight that I love to know.

    You are a sight to behold
    A beauty that can't be told
    Your branches a canopy
    A comforting sight to see.

    You are a symbol of strength
    A sight that is great length
    Your roots deep and true
    A sight that is so true.

You are a sight of peace and tranquillity
    A sight that brings a sense of calm
    You are a sight that soothes the soul
    A sight that can do no harm.

You are a sight of grace and poise
A sight that never loses its charm
You are a sight that never fades
A sight that is always full of charm.

So, here's to you, dear willow tree
With your branches so long and free
You are a sight that I love to see
A symbol of strength and serenity.

You are a sight that will always be
A part of me and my memory
A sight that brings me joy and peace
A sight that will never cease.

So, thank you, dear willow tree
For all the beauty you bring
You are a sight that I am grateful for
A sight that makes my heart sing.

The Wrath of Mother Nature

The Wrath of Mother Nature, a force to be reckoned with
A power beyond measure, a tempestuous fit
She rages and roars, with wind and with rain
A tempestuous goddess, causing much pain.

Her fury is feared by all who behold
The destruction she wreaks leaves stories untold
She lashes out with no mercy or grace
Leaving behind ruin in her path's trace.

Yet, despite all her anger and all her despair
She is also a wonder beyond compare
For even in rage, she is a sight to behold
A force of great power to be reckoned with, so bold.

So, let us respect her and all that she gives
For even in wrath, she has much left to live
For she is a goddess, a force of great might
The Wrath of Mother Nature, a terrifying sight.

So, let us be mindful and heed her great call
For even in rage, she is a force of it all
For she is the Earth and all that she gives
The Wrath of Mother Nature, a force to be reckoned with.

An Idiot Without Remorse

There once was an idiot so dense
He lacked common sense, that was immense
He acted with no remorse
Leaving those around him to endorse.

His foolish behaviour with a defence
He strutted through life with a lack of care
Ignoring all those who stood and stared
He thought himself quite clever and smart.

But in reality, he was just an idiot at heart
He laughed at the pain and strife
Of those whose lives he helped entwine
He revelled in the chaos he'd caused.

Leaving a trail of destruction, not pausing to pause
But karma has a way of catching up
And the idiot soon found himself in a rut
His actions had consequences; it turns out.

And he was left with nothing, no doubt
So let this be a lesson to all
Who may think themselves above it all
Karma will come, it's only a matter of time
And the idiot will be left behind.

Lost Friends

Oh, lost friends, how I miss you so
The bond we shared I'll never let go
But fate has torn us apart
And left me with a broken heart.

I remember the times we laughed and played
The memories we made
I remember the joy and the fun
The love that we had won.

But now you are gone and I am left behind
Feeling lost and alone, with a heart that is intertwined
With pain and with sorrow, with grief and with woe
Wishing you were still here and not letting go.

I miss your smile and your laugh
The way we used to chat
I miss the way we used to be
Together, wild and free.

I miss the way we used to hang out
And the way we used to shout
I miss the way we used to share
Our hopes, our dreams and our cares.

But I know that you are watching over me
From above, with love and with care
I know that you are proud of me
And that you are always there.

I know that you are at peace
And that you have been released
From the pain and the suffering
And the troubles that life can bring.

So, I will hold on to the memories
Of all the times we shared
And I will hold on to the love
That we both always bared.

I will cherish the moments we had
The moments that were so rad
And I will keep them close to my heart
And never let them part.

And I will be strong and I will carry on
For I know that is what you would want me to do
I will live my life to the fullest
In honour of you.

For you are my friends and I am yours
Forever and always, we will be bound
By the love that we shared
And the memories that we found.

So, rest in peace, dear friends
And know that I will always love you
You will always be in my heart
Forever and ever, through and through.

I may not be able to see you
Or hold you close to me
But I will always feel your presence
And the love that you bring to me.

So, here's to you, dear friends
The ones who mean the world to me
The ones who have always been there
The ones I love and miss endlessly.

Grandmother...

Oh, grandmother, with your wrinkled face
And your greying hair in its rightful place
You may be old, but you are wise
And full of tales and full of surprises.

You may be slow, but you are steady
And always ready for a good story
You may be set in your ways
But you always know just what to say.

You may not be up to date
With the latest fashion or technological plate
But you are wise beyond your years
And full of laughter and full of cheer.

You may not be able to keep up
With the fast pace of the modern world
But you are a treasure and a delight
And a source of love and a source of light.

So, here's to you, dear grandmother
With your wrinkled face and your greying hair
You may be old, but you are wise
And always ready for a good time and a good scare.

Subjectification

Subjectification a force that shapes our lives
It defines who we are and who we strive to be
It influences our thoughts, our actions and our dreams
It determines our place in society, or so it seems.

It tells us what to value, what to believe
It shapes our identity and how we perceive
Ourselves and others in this world we live
It can lift us up, or it can make us feel small and misgive.

But we must remember that we have agency
We can choose to defy subjectification and be free
To define ourselves and live our truth
To resist the forces that seek to shape our youth.

We are more than just subjects; we are people with hearts and minds
We have the power to shape our own lives and be kind
To ourselves and others, no matter what society may say
We are all deserving of love and respect every single day.

So let us reject subjectification and embrace our true selves
Let us live authentically and put our worries on the shelves
For we are all unique and that is something to be celebrated
Let us embrace our individuality and be greatly elated.

The Woman I Hope to One Day Call My Wife

She stands before me like a work of art
A masterpiece, a vision of grace
Her beauty like a beacon, a shining star
A sight that leaves my heart in its place.

Her curves are like a symphony
A harmony of lines and shape
She is a goddess of elegance and mystery
A woman who can make my heart escape.

Her eyes are pools of liquid gold
Reflecting the light within
She is a story yet untold
A mystery, I long to begin.

Her voice is like a lullaby
A soothing melody that calms
She is a woman who can make me fly
A treasure in her arms.

Her touch is like a fire
A burning passion, a desire
She is a love that will never tire
A woman who can light my entire fire.

Her laughter echoes like a bell
A sweet sound, a music to my ears
She is a woman who can make me dwell
In a world of happiness and cheers.

She walks with a poise like a queen
A ruler of her own fate
She is a woman who can make me lean
On her, to never be late.

She is a breath of fresh air
A soothing breeze, a refreshing change
She is a woman who can make me stare
In awe at her beauty, that's never strange.

She is a work of art, an inspiration
A muse that guides my every move
She is a woman of pure sensation
A love that I am blessed to prove.

She is a rose among the thorns
A beauty that stands out
She is a woman who can make me mourn
If ever she were to fade out.

She is a ray of sunshine
A light that shines so bright
She is a woman who can make me pine
For her, day and night.

She is a treasure, a diamond
A precious gem in the rough
She is a woman who can make me stand
Tall, proud and never tough.

She is a song, a melody
A music that plays in my head
She is a woman who can make me see
A love that's worth more than pure gold.

She is a dream, a fantasy
A vision that comes true
She is a woman who can make me believe
In a love that's pure and true.

She is a mystery, an enigma
A puzzle yet to unfold
She is a woman who can make me wanna
Know her, stories untold.

She is a story, a novel
A tale that's worth a read
She is a woman who can make me revel
In a love that's pure and said.

She is a gift, a blessing
A treasure that's worth the wait
She is a woman who can make me sing
Of a love, that's truly great.

She is a woman of elegance and poise
A goddess, a beauty to behold
She is a woman who can make me rejoice
In a love that's pure and bold.

She is the one, my everything
A love that's worth all the while
She is a woman who can make me sing
Of a love that's truly mine.

I Am Not a Sailor; I Am a Tugboat Operator

I am not a sailor; I am a tugboat operator
Steering through the ports with a steady hand and focus
Guiding ships in and out with precision and care
I am the unsung hero of this maritime affair.

My vessel may be small, but my role is vital
I am the backbone of this bustling port terminal
With my powerful engines, I tow and push
Ensuring the safe passage of every vessel and hush.

I may not sail the seas like the grand ships do
But my job is just as important, in this world so blue
I keep the traffic flowing with skill and might
I am the tugboat operator, a true maritime knight.

I work in all weathers, through storms and swell
I am the unsung hero who keeps the ports well
I may not be glamorous, but my work is done with pride
I am the tugboat operator on whom ships rely and confide.

I may not be a sailor, but I am a sailor' friend
I help their journey, from beginning to the end
I am the unsung hero of this aquatic scene
I am the tugboat operator, the backbone of this marine.

I may not have the freedom of a sailor on the sea
But I have a purpose and that's enough for me
I am the unsung hero of this nautical industry
I am the tugboat operator, the backbone of this economy.

I may not be the star of this maritime show
But my work is essential and that's all I need to know
I am the unsung hero of this aquatic realm
I am the tugboat operator at the helm.

So next time you see a tugboat chugging through the bay
Remember the operator, who works hard day by day
We may not be sailors, but we are the ones who keep the ships on track
We are the unsung heroes of this maritime act.

Dear Hippy…

Oh, hippy, with your flowered crown
and your peaceful ways, up and down
You spread love and joy far and wide
and let your spirit freely glide.

You live life to the fullest with no regret
and let your heart and your mind never be met
With negativity or hate
But only with love and fate.

You embrace nature and all its might
and let your soul take flight
You are free and wild and full of grace
and bring a smile to every face.

So, here's to you, dear hippy
With your flowered crown and your peaceful way
You spread love and joy far and wide
and let your spirit freely glide.

You are a reminder of a simpler time
when love and peace were all that mattered
You are a light in a world that is dark
and a source of hope that can never be barred.

So, keep on living, dear hippy
With your flowered crown and your peaceful way
and know that you are loved
For all that you do and all that you say.

A Grey Cloud

Oh, grey cloud, with your gloomy cloak
You bring a sense of sadness and a sense of despair
You obscure the light and the warmth of the sun
And leave behind a feeling of unease and a feeling of undone.

But despite your sombre appearance
You bring something more, something dear
You bring the rain and the nourishment it brings
You bring the life that the earth so needs.

You are a reminder of the cycles of life
Of the ups and the downs and the highs and the strife
You are a reminder that everything has its place
And that every cloud has a silver lining and a saving grace.

You are a force of nature's power
A force that can shower
The earth with life and with renewal
A force that is vital and crucial.

You may bring sadness, but you also bring hope
You may bring darkness, but you also bring scope
For new beginnings and for new growth
For a chance to start anew and to shed the old.

So, here's to you, dear grey cloud
With your gloomy cloak and your sombre shroud
You may bring sadness, but you also bring life
And for that, you are worth the strife.

You are a reminder that even in the darkest of days
There is always a way to find the light
To find the hope and to find the strength
To keep going and to find the length.

You are a reminder that change is constant
And that nothing stays the same
You are a reminder that life is a journey
And that it is up to us to claim.

You are a reminder of the beauty in the world
Of the beauty in the rain and the beauty unfurled
In the petals of a flower and in the leaves of a tree
In the laughter of a child and in the love of family.

You are a reminder that beauty can be found
In the most unexpected places and in the most unexpected sounds
So, thank you, dear grey cloud, for all that you bring
For the beauty and for the hope and for the love that you bring.

New Year's Day...

Oh, New Year's Day, a time of new beginnings
A time to leave the old behind and to embrace new winnings
A time to set goals and to make resolutions
A time to start anew and to find solutions.

A time to reflect on the year that has passed
A time to be grateful for the moments that have lasted
A time to learn from the mistakes we have made
A time to grow and to be unafraid.

A time to be hopeful and to dream big
A time to be ambitious and to give it a dig
A time to be bold and to take a chance
A time to be fearless and to advance.

So, here's to New Year's Day, a time of new beginnings
A time to leave the old behind and to embrace new winnings
A time to be hopeful and to dream big
A time to be fearless and to give it a dig.
Happy New Year!

Bully's

Bullying is a cruel and harmful deed
It makes others feel like they don't belong, like they're not wanted, like they're not needed
But we must remember every soul is worthy, every heart is pure
and we all deserve to feel secure.

Bullying can come in many forms, from physical abuse to verbal taunts
It can make us feel small and insignificant like we don't amount
But we must rise above the hate and negativity
And show the world our true identity.

We must stand up for ourselves and others
And let bullies know that their actions are not proper
We must show them that kindness and respect are key
And that hurting others is not okay, not okay to be.

We must remember that we are all unique and special
And that every one of us has a potential
So, let's come together and make a stand
And make bullying a problem we can dismantle.

Let's spread love and acceptance everywhere we go
And let bullying know that it's time for it to go
We are all in this together; let's make a plan
And put an end to bullying in our land.

Heartbreak

Heartbreak, it cuts like a knife
It leaves a wound that takes a lifetime to heal.
It fills us with pain and endless strife
And makes us feel like we can't go on like we can't deal.

We thought our love was strong and true
But it crumbled and fell apart, just like a sandcastle.
We thought we had a bond that nothing could undo
But we were wrong and now we're left to handle.

We try to move on and let go
But the memories linger like a ghost.
We try to fill the void and mend the hole
But the hurt is always there; it never goes.

We wonder what went wrong and where we failed
We replay the past and blame ourselves
We wonder if we could've done something different
If we could've saved the love that was once our wealth.

But sometimes love just isn't enough
Sometimes, things just don't work out.
And all we can do is accept and move on
Even though it feels like there's a constant drought.

Heartbreak is a journey that we all must take
It's a part of life and the human experience.
But we must remember that we are strong and capable
And that we will find love and happiness.

So, let's hold our heads up high and be brave
And let the heartbreak make us stronger.
Let's open our hearts to new beginnings and new love
And let the past be a lesson, not a weight on our shoulder.

Monday Mornings

Monday mornings, oh, how I dread
The alarm clock's ring fills me with dread
I drag myself out of bed
Wishing I could stay in my warm cocoon instead.

The weekend was too short, it flew by
And now, it's back to the grind; time to try
To put on a brave face and face the day
But deep down inside, I just want to stay.

The thought of going to work fills me with sorrow
I wish I could stay in bed until tomorrow
But bills won't pay themselves; I must rise
And put on a smile, even though inside, I want to die.

Monday mornings, they always come too soon
Leaving me feeling empty and alone
But I'll get through it like I always do
Hoping that the weekend comes back into view.

A Crusader like Me

A Crusader, proud and brave
A warrior of the Holy Land
With sword in hand and heart ablaze
He fights for God and his holy cause.

He rides forth on his mighty steed
Defending the kingdom and those in need
No challenge too great, no foe too strong
He fights on, driven by faith and purpose.

Through battles, fierce and hard trials
He stands firm, a shining guard
Defying death and embracing fate
He fights on a Crusader of great.

He is a symbol of courage and strength
A defender of the weak and the meek
He is a warrior of honour and valour
A Crusader, a hero to all.

He has faced countless dangers and foes
But he never falters; he never slows
He stands tall and fights with all his might
A Crusader, a beacon of light.

His name will live on through the ages
A hero of the Christian faith
A shining light in the darkest times
A Crusader, forever in our hearts and minds.

So let us honour and remember KamilKazie
The brave Crusader, a hero forever
May his legacy inspire us all
To be strong and brave and stand tall.

The Righteous Executioner

A righteous executioner walks alone
In a world that shuns his chosen path
He is a man of justice, skin of stone
And a heart that feels the weight of wrath.

He bears the burden of taking life
With a solemn duty and heavy hand
He knows the cost; he pays the price
For he understands the moral stand.

He stands tall and proud, a guardian of order
A protector of the innocent and weak
He wields his sword with pride and valour
And the guilty tremble at his feet.

His task is not one of pleasure or joy
But of necessity and reason's call
He spares no mercy for the destroyer
But offers a peaceful end to all.

He is a man of honour and of law
A servant of the higher good
A guardian of the gates, a keeper of the door
A guardian of the neighbourhood.

He is the balance in a world gone mad
A beacon of hope in darkest night
He is the executioner, a righteous man
A shining example of what is right.

So let those who would seek to do harm
Beware the righteous executioner's might
For he will stand tall, a guardian of the peace
A guardian of the eternal light.

Curious Stranger

I wonder about you, dear stranger
I wonder about your life and your past
I wonder about your struggles and triumphs
I wonder about the choices you've made at last.

I wonder about your family and friends
I wonder about the people you hold dear
I wonder about your hopes and dreams
I wonder about the path you hold dear.

I wonder about your passions and hobbies
I wonder about the things that make you shine
I wonder about your challenges and challenges
I wonder about the struggles that are yours and mine.

I wonder about your triumphs and failures
I wonder about the lessons that you've learned
I wonder about the person that you are
I wonder about the person that you've earned.

I wonder about your past and future
I wonder about the road you've travelled on
I wonder about the person that you'll become
I wonder about the path that you'll find dawn.

I wonder about your secrets and your stories
I wonder about the tales that you could tell
I wonder about the person that you hide
I wonder about the person that you'll sell.

I wonder about you, dear stranger
I wonder about your life and your past
I wonder about the mysteries that you hold
I wonder about the secrets that will last.

My .50 Cal Gun

My .50 Cal gun, a mighty beast
A weapon of war, a gun of the elite
It towers above all others
A symbol of power, a gun for the bold.

With a round as big as your thumb
It packs a punch that's sure to numb
It can take out a truck or a plane
It can cause destruction; it knows no shame.

But with great power comes great responsibility
And the .50 Cal gun is no exception
It must be handled with care and respect
For it has the power to cause great destruction.

So let us remember, as we hold this gun
That it is not a toy, it is not for fun
It is a tool of war, a tool of death
And it must be treated with caution, with every breath.

The Devil's Snare

The Devil's Snare, a wicked plant
It wraps its vines around the heart
It strangles and suffocates
It tears us apart.

It lures us in with its seductive charms
It promises pleasure, it promises delight
But it's all a lie, a cruel deception
It's a trap, a snare, a deadly sight.

It entangles us in its web of lies
It twists and turns; it never stops
It drains us of our energy, our strength
It feeds on our weaknesses; it feeds on our thoughts.

It consumes us; it takes us over
It becomes the master of our soul
It drags us down to the depths of darkness
It takes control; it takes its toll.

But we must resist, we must fight
We must break free from its hold
We must find the courage and the strength
To be bold, to be whole.

We must shatter the chains that bind us
We must cut the vines that strangle our hearts
We must reclaim our power, our freedom
We must break the Devil's Snare and start.

So let us rise, let us shine
Let us break free from the darkness
Let us find the courage and the strength
To escape the Devil's Snare and embrace the light.

A Lustful Man

He is a man of lust and desire
A man consumed by his passions
He is hopelessly in love with love
And he craves the touch of another.

He is a man of endless need
A man who can never be satisfied
He is constantly searching for more
And he is driven by his primal side.

He is a man of endless temptation
A man who is drawn to the forbidden
He is a slave to his own desires
And he is unable to control his cravings.

He is a man of endless yearning
A man who is always looking for something new
He is never satisfied with what he has
And he is constantly seeking something new.

He is a man of endless longing
A man who is always searching for the next best thing
He is driven by his own lust
And he is unable to find true happiness.

He is a man of endless frustration
A man who is always chasing an elusive dream
He is trapped in his own desires
And he is unable to break free from the chains of his own lust.

He is a man of endless sorrow
A man who is always left wanting more
He is trapped in a cycle of longing and desire
And he is unable to find true love or happiness.

He is a man of endless regret
A man who is haunted by his own mistakes
He is trapped in a cycle of lust and desire
And he is unable to break free from the chains that bind him.

A Refugee I Know

She was a refugee, forced to flee her home
Leaving behind all that she knew
She was just a girl with a heart full of hope
But the world was cruel and it broke her in two.

She travelled far, across land and sea
Searching for a place to call her own
She braved the dangers, the dangers unseen
Hoping to find a place to call home.

She encountered many hardships along the way
But she refused to give up or give in
She kept on going through the darkest of days
Hoping to find a place where she could begin.

She finally found it, a place of love and light
A place where she could heal and grow
She found a home, a place to belong
A place where she could let her spirit flow.

She blossomed there, like a flower in the sun
She flourished and thrived; she shone bright.
She found her strength, her courage, her voice
And she let her light shine, day and night.

She became a leader, an inspiration to all
A beacon of hope, a shining star
She stood tall and she never looked back
She knew that she had come so very far.

She was a refugee, but she found her way
She found a place to call her own.
She found love and light and she found her strength
And she knew that she was finally home.

A Homeless Man

He was a man of homelessness
A man with no place to call his own
He wandered the streets, day and night
Searching for a place to call home.

He had no family, no friends
No one to turn to in his time of need
He was alone in the world
With nothing but his thoughts to guide him indeed.

But he never lost hope
He never lost faith in the world
He knew that one day, things would turn around
And his luck would finally be unfurled.

He worked hard every day
Doing whatever he could to survive
He was a survivor, a fighter
He refused to give in; he refused to dive.

And one day, his luck finally changed
He found a place to call his own
He found a home, a place of love and light
A place where he could heal and grow.

He blossomed there like a flower in the sun
He flourished and thrived; he shone bright
He found his strength, his courage, his voice
And he let his light shine, day and night.

He became a leader, an inspiration to all
A beacon of hope, a shining star
He stood tall and he never looked back
He knew that he had come so very far.

He was a man of homelessness
But he found his way; he found his home
He found love and light and he found his strength
And he knew that he was finally home.

Ruthless Love

There once was a man, oh so fine
Whose love was as fierce as a venomous vine
He would stop at nothing, no matter the cost
To win over the heart of the one he loved most.

He was cunning and sly, a master of deceit
He'd manipulate and charm with words so sweet
He'd do whatever it took, no matter the toll
For the love of his life, he'd give up his soul.

But she was a woman, strong and true
She saw through his lies and his love, she eschewed
For she knew in her heart that true love was pure
And his ruthless pursuit could never endure.

But the man he was stubborn and refused to give in
He was blinded by love and his ego did win
He pursued her still, with a passion so bold
But she stood her ground and his love, she would not hold.

For she knew in her heart that love should be kind
And the man who stood before her was only one of a kind
He was ruthless and selfish and his love was not true
And so, with a heavy heart, she bid him adieu.

But the man, he did not give up and continued to chase
He was determined to win and win her embrace
But she was not swayed and her heart remained pure
And so, in the end, his love, she did demure.

For true love is patient and kind and true
And the man who stood before her was not the one for her to pursue
She moved on and found love that was real
And the man he was left with the pain of her heel.

So, beware of the man who will stop at nothing
To win over the love of the one he's pursuing
For true love is selfless and kind and true
And the man who loves only himself is not the one for you.

The Colours of the Rainbow

The rainbow is a symphony of colours
A canvas of hues that dance and play
From red, so bold and vibrant
To purple, so regal and royal, it's a sight to stay.

Red, like a flame that burns with passion and fire
Is a colour of love, a colour of desire
Orange, so warm and sunny
Brings a ray of happiness on a bright summer's day.

Yellow, so cheerful and bright
Brings a ray of sunshine on a cold winter's day
Green, so peaceful and serene
Fills the soul with peace, like the grass on a rolling hill.

Blue, so calm and tranquil
Soothes the mind and soul, like the ocean waves
Indigo, a colour of mystery and depth
Brings a sense of intrigue, a sense of mystery to the mix.

Purple, so regal and royal
Brings a sense of grandeur, like a precious gem
It's a colour of creativity, a colour of imagination
A colour that inspires the mind to wander and explore.

The rainbow is a symphony of colours
A canvas of hues that dance and play
From red to purple and all the shades in between
It's a splash of magic, a splash of wonder, every day.

So let us embrace the colours of the rainbow
Let us appreciate their beauty and their hue
For each colour brings something special to the mix
A splash of magic, a splash of wonder, just for you.

The rainbow is a symbol of hope and love
A symbol of promise, a symbol of new beginnings
So let us embrace it and all its colours
And let its magic fill our hearts and our souls with endless love and endless joy.

The Four Seasons

The seasons come and go, with the passing of time
Bringing new life, new beginnings
From the icy grip of winter
To the warm embrace of summer, the cycle never ends.

Winter, with its snowy blankets
And its frosty winds that howl and moan
It's a time of rest, a time of solitude
A time to huddle close to the hearth and stay warm.

Spring, with its gentle showers
And its green shoots that peek through the soil
It's a time of renewal, a time of growth
A time to awaken from the long winter's toil.

Summer, with its sunny days
And it's lazy, hazy afternoons
It's a time of fun, a time of joy
A time to soak up the sun and make the most of every moment.

Fall, with its golden leaves
And it's crisp, cool air that invigorates the soul
It's a time of harvest, a time of abundance
A time to give thanks and to make the most of every goal.

Each season has its own charm, its own magic
Each one brings something special to the mix
From the icy grip of winter
To the warm embrace of summer, the cycle never ends.

The seasons change with the passing of time
Bringing new life, new beginnings
From the gentle showers of spring
To the golden leaves of fall, the cycle never ends.

The seasons are a reminder of the passage of time
A reminder that nothing stays the same
So let us make the most of every moment
And let us appreciate the beauty of each season in its own unique way.

Let us embrace the seasons
And all that they bring
Let us appreciate the beauty of each one
And let us make the most of every day.

Food My Love

I love the way it smells and tastes
It's always there when I feel low
It fills my heart with joy and cheer
For food, my love will never wane and go.

Each bite is a treasure to savour
A burst of flavour in my mouth
It satisfies my every craving
And fills me up without a doubt.

I love to try new dishes and cuisines
To discover new flavours and ways to dine
Food is a source of endless pleasure
It always puts a smile on my face, divine.

From the sizzle of a steak on the grill
To the aroma of freshly baked bread
Food is a source of endless thrill
It fills my senses ahead.

I love to cook and bake with care
To share my love with others, I dare
Food brings people together
It's a source of love, comfort and cheer.

From the first light of dawn
To the dead of night
I crave for food, a constant pawn
It brings me endless delight.

So here's to food, my one true love
A source of joy that I'll always treasure
I'll eat and eat and eat some more
For food, my love will never measure.

Coffee

There's something about the aroma
It fills my senses from head to toe
It wakes me up and energises
My love for coffee it continues to grow.

Each cup is a moment of pleasure,
A warm embrace in the morning's cold
It soothes my nerves and calms my soul
My love for coffee it never grows old.

I love the way it tastes and feels
A perfect blend of flavours and beans
It gives me strength and makes me real
My love for coffee it runs deep within.

From a simple drip to a fancy latte
I'll take it anyway, I don't discriminate
Coffee is my ultimate comfort
My love for it, I can't abdicate.

I love to try new roasts and blends
To discover new flavours and friends
Coffee is a source of endless wonder
My love for it, it will never surrender.

So, here's to coffee, my one true love
A source of joy that I'll always treasure
I'll drink and drink and drink some more
For coffee, my love will never measure.

Hopeless Romantic

A hopeless romantic, full of love and light
A heart on fire, burning bright
He searched the world from near and far
For the one he knew would be his shining star.

He waited patiently through joy and pain
For the day, he could call her his and never part again
But alas, love does not always go as planned
And though his heart may break, it will never be unmanned.

For even in darkness, he holds on to hope
That someday, his love will help him cope
A hopeless romantic, forever true
His love will conquer all and make his dreams come true.

He reads her favourite poetry, writes her love letters every day
He sings her sweet ballads in his own special way
He brings her flowers just because he cares
He shows her love and kindness beyond compare.

He holds her close and kisses her gentle lips
He tells her he loves her with every single wish
A hopeless romantic, through and through
He'll love her forever, his love so true.

He'll stand by her side through thick and thin
He'll be her rock and let her know he'll always win
For she is his everything, his reason for being
He'll love her with all his heart and never stop believing
A hopeless romantic until the end of time
He'll love her with all his might, his love so fine.

The Big Day

The wedding day a momentous occasion
Two hearts joined together in love's fusion
The bride is beautiful in her flowing gown
The groom stands tall, with pride aboundg.

The ceremony is filled with love and joy
As the couple exchange vows, they both employ
The rings they wear a symbol of their devotion
A lifelong promise, a love with emotion.

The reception is full of laughter and cheer
As the newlywed's dance, without any fear
Their love is strong as they start their new life
Together forever, as husband and wife
The wedding day, a celebration grand
A beautiful beginning for the love at hand.

The Winds of Love

The winds of change, they blow so strong
As we say goodbye to what has gone
The memories we shared; they fill our hearts
But now it's time for us to part.

The paths we take may lead us far
But love remains a shining star
It guides us through the darkest night
And gives us strength to face the fight.

We'll look back on the times we had
And smile through tears of joy and sad
For though we go, our love remains
A bond so strong it breaks all chains.

So, let us hold on to the past
But look ahead to what will last
For love endures through time and space
A never-ending fire we'll embrace.

A Wandering Wonderer

A wandering wonderer with thoughts so deep
He wanders through life in search of sleep
He wonders and wonders as he travels far
What his purpose is and who he are.

He wonders about love and what it means
He wonders about life and all its scenes
He wonders about the world and all its charms
He wonders about the future and all its alarms.

He wonders and wonders as he walks the earth
In search of answers and a newfound mirth
But in the end, he knows it doesn't matter
For in his heart, love will always shatter
The walls he's built and set him free
To wander and wonder endlessly.

A Head-on Fire

A head-on fire, burning bright
Filled with thoughts, both day and night
A mind so vast, with endless ideas
It never stops, it never tires.

A head-on fire, so full of passion
It drives you forward with its fashion
It fuels your dreams and helps them grow
It sets your soul aglow.

A head-on fire, a burning flame
It guides you through life's endless game
It sparks your creativity and sets you apart
It helps you see the beauty in art.

A head-on fire, a brilliant light
It illuminates your darkest night
So let your head burn, with all its might
And never let your flame lose sight.

A Double-Edged Knife

A double edge knife, a deadly tool
It cuts through life with its sharpened rule
It can bring harm or offer aid
It all depends on how it's wielded, the blade.

A double edge knife, a symbol of power
It can protect, in darkest hour
But it can also bring destruction and pain
It all depends on the one who holds the reigns.

A double edge knife, a two-sided coin
It can bring peace or endless toil
It all depends on the hand that holds
The power to choose between good and old.

A double edge knife, a dangerous tool
It must be used with caution and rule
For it can bring both joy and strife
It all depends on the hand and the life.

Ruthless and Relentless Woman I Love

She strides through life with purpose and might
A force to be reckoned with, day and night
Her resolve is unbreakable, her will unwavering
She never falters, never wavering.

Her tongue is sharp as a razor's edge
She cuts through lies and deceit with ease
Her words are weapons wielded with care
She wields them skilfully, never baring.

Her heart is cold as ice, hard as stone
Love and compassion have left her alone
She tramples on the weak and the meek
Their pleas for mercy fall on deaf ears, unheard.

But still, I love to hate this ruthless, relentless woman
For even in her cruelty, there is something human
A glimmer of vulnerability, a hint of fear
That keeps me coming back, year after year.

I can't help but admire her strength and might
Even as I cringe at the thought of her sight
She is a paradox, a mystery, an enigma wrapped in riddle
But one thing is for certain: she is no simple little.

So, I'll continue to love to hate this ruthless, relentless woman
For as long as she struts through life, unyielding and inhuman
For in her strength and cruelty, I see a reflection of myself
A reminder of the power we all hold, to love and to hate, to save or to condemn.

Dying Christmas Tree

Once a mighty spruce, tall and proud
It stood tall, a Christmas crowd
But now it lies, withered and dry
A victim of time left to die.

It should have been in a pot, safe and sound
To be replanted on higher ground
But instead, it was left to decay
A forgotten soul on Christmas day.

The lights that once shone bright and bold
Are now dim, their lustre grown old
The ornaments, once shiny and new
Are now tarnished, their colours askew.

But even in death, the tree stands tall
A reminder of Christmases, past and all
Of laughter and love, of cheer and cheer
It will be missed, this dying tree, next year.

Naughty Child

There once was a child full of cheer
But oh, how he loved to cause fear
He'd sneak and he'd sneak, with nary a sound
Leaving his parents spinning round and round.

He'd pull all the pots from the kitchen shelf
He'd climb up the curtains for a laugh and a guff
He'd draw on the walls with markers and crayons
Leaving his parents tired and drained.

But through it all, the parents held on
For they knew deep down their naughty son
Was just full of love and mischief and play
And one day, he'd grow up in a better way.

So, they took it all in stride, the spills and the messes
For they knew their naughty child was just testing limits and boundaries
And one day, he'd grow up to be kind and true
And they'd look back, on these days, with love and fond memories, too.

So, don't give up, dear parents, of a naughty child
For with patience and love, they'll grow up wild and free
Just hold on tight and guide them through
And one day, they'll turn out just fine, as can be.

Depression

Depression, a heavy weight that bears down
Dragging us into darkness, lost and found
A constant battle that we fight within
But we must remember, we're not alone in this.

It's okay to feel the pain and let it show
To cry and scream and let the hurt flow
It's okay to take a break and rest a while
To gather strength and mend the wounds that pile.

But don't give up, don't let go
There is a light that shines, you must know
A love that warms, a hope that glows
A future bright if only you let it grow.

So, reach out, seek help and don't be afraid
To share your pain and the burdens you've made
For there are those who care and understand
Who will hold your hand and lend a helping hand.

You are strong, you are brave
You have the power to rise from the grave
To heal and thrive, to love and live
To find the joy and all that life can give.

So, hold on tight and don't let go
For better days are surely on the horizon, don't you know?
And though the journey may be rough and long
You are not alone; you are loved and belong.

The Pet I Love

My dear and faithful friend
With you until the very end
Your presence brought me joy and light
Helping me through the darkest nights.

But now your time on earth is through
Leaving me with a heart so true
But heavy with grief and filled with pain
Wondering how I'll live without you again.

I'll never forget the happy times we shared
The adventures we took, the love we declared
You were always there, by my side
A loyal companion, my joy and pride.

But now you're gone and I am left
To mourn the loss, to feel the heft
Of your absence, a gaping hole
That no one else can ever fill or console.

I'll miss your wagging tail, your soft fur coat
The way you'd curl up on my lap and gloat
In the love and affection I'd give
For as long as you lived.

But now you're gone and I am here
Alone and lost, with nothing to hold dear
But the memories of you that I'll keep
Close to my heart, forever asleep.

Rest in peace, my beloved pet
I'll love you always and never forget
The joy and love you brought to my life
You'll always be a part of it through joy and strife.

A Ghost from the Past

A ghost from the past, a shadow of the past
Returning to haunt me, the memories cast
A reminder of the hurt and pain
Of the love that died, the ties that wane.

But why now? Why haunt me this way?
Why bring back the ghosts of yesterday?
The wounds that healed, the scars that fade
The love that died, the heart that strayed.

I thought I moved on; I thought I let go
I thought I found peace and learned to grow
But here you are, a ghost from the past
Bringing back the memories that last.

I try to push you away, to banish the ghost
But you keep coming back, no matter how I boast
Of my strength and resilience, of my will to survive
You keep coming back, keeping me alive.

And so, I face you, the ghost from the past
I face my fears and the pain that lasts
I confront the memories and the love that died
I confront the hurt and the tears I've cried.

And as I do, I realise with a start
That the ghost from the past is a part of my heart
A part of my journey, a part of my growth
A part of the person I've become, I know.

So, I embrace the ghost, the shadow of the past
I embrace the memories and make them last
I learn from the love and the hurt and the pain
And I carry them with me as I move on again.

For the ghost from the past is not a curse
But a blessing in disguise, a gift, not a hearse
It teaches me, it guides me, it helps me to see
The person I am and the person I can be.

Cold Shiver

A cold shiver, a chill down the spine
A sensation that lingers, a feeling divine
A sign of fear, or a sign of thrill
A response to danger or a response to chill.

But what is a cold shiver, really and truly
A mere physical response, or something more ethereal?
Is it a message from the body or the soul
A warning, or a wonder, or a goal?

Perhaps it is a reminder of our primal past
A memory of danger that still holds fast
A reminder of the threats that once roamed the land
A reminder of the fears that still grip our hands.

Or perhaps it is a glimpse of something beyond
A peek into the mysteries of the unknown
A hint of the infinite, the eternal, the divine
A spark of the soul that shines and intertwines.

For the cold shiver is not just a sensation
But a reflection of the human condition
It reveals our depth, our complexity, our range
It captures the essence of the human change.

So next time you feel a cold shiver down your spine
Don't just brush it off as a mere design
Embrace it, explore it, let it guide your way
For it may lead you to a deeper understanding of the human say.

Sweet Little House Mouse

There once was a mouse who lived in a house
A tiny little creature full of mouse charm and mouse grace
He scurried and scattered from place to place
Leaving behind a trail of mouse footsteps and mouse traces.

But he wasn't just any mouse, no sir
He was a mouse with personality
He was curious and brave and oh-so-clever
He was the mouse that everyone wanted to treasure.

He'd sneak into the pantry in the dead of night
And nibble on the cheese with all his might
He'd sneak into the bedroom and dance on the bed
Leaving behind a mess that would leave you for dead.

But despite his mischief, he was loved by all
For he brought joy and laughter when he'd scurry and crawl
So, if you ever see a mouse in your house or your home
Don't be afraid; embrace it and make it your own.

For a mouse is a gift, a blessing in disguise
A creature full of wonder and mouse-like surprise
So, don't be afraid of the mouse in your house
Embrace it, love it and let it be your mouse spouse.

Blood Brother

A bond forged in crimson, a bond that will last
Through trials and triumphs, forever steadfast
Through battles and hardships, through joy and through pain
Our bond remains unbroken through sunshine and rain.

With you by my side, I know I can face
Any challenge that comes with courage and grace
Your strength is my own; your courage is mine
Together, we are unstoppable, a power divine.

Our bond is a bond of loyalty and love
A bond that will never, ever be undone
A bond that will carry us through thick and through thin
Our bond is a bond that will always win.

Through good times and bad, we stand shoulder-to-shoulder
Through laughter and tears, we are one and we'll always be
Through triumph and defeat, we face every challenge as one
Our bond is unbreakable till our journey is done.

We are brothers by blood, but more than that, too
We are brothers in spirit, through and through
Our bond is a bond of love and respect
A bond that will keep us close, even when we're apart.

So, here's to you, my Blood Brother, my friend
May our bond never weaken until the very end
And even beyond that, into eternity
Our bond will remain, a bond of unity.

Our bond is unbreakable; it will never fade
It will always stay strong through any raid
We are brothers forever, through thick and through thin
Our bond is a bond that will always win.

A Resurrected Soul

A soul once lost now found
A heart once broken, now sound
A spirit once shattered now whole
A resurrected soul.

From the ashes of pain and despair
A new being emerges, beyond compare
Stronger and wiser, filled with light
A resurrected soul, ready to take flight.

Gone are the chains that once held it down
Gone is the darkness, replaced by a crown
Of hope and redemption, of love and of grace
A resurrected soul, ready to embrace.

This new life, filled with endless possibilities
A chance to start over, to break free from responsibilities
To follow one's dreams, to chase one's heart
A resurrected soul, ready to restart.

But this journey is not without its struggles and fears
As the road ahead is filled with unknowns and tears
Yet through it all, the soul remains resilient
For it has been resurrected and it is plentiful.

So, here's to the resurrected soul; may it flourish and grow
May it spread its wings and let its light show
May it rise above all obstacles and strife
And continue to shine throughout this life.

For the resurrected soul is a force to be reckoned with
It is a beacon of hope, a source of strength and myth
It is a reminder that no matter how low we may fall
We can always rise again and stand tall.

A Time Approaching

As the shadows lengthen and the evening hues
Begin to paint the sky with vibrant hues
I find myself lost in thought, gazing afar
At the time approaching, so bright and bizarre.

For the future is a mysterious thing
A canvas waiting to be painted, a song waiting to sing
It holds within it endless possibilities
Paths yet to be taken, adventures yet to be seized.

But as the time approaches, I find myself torn
Between fear and excitement, between doubt and adorn
For the unknown can be a daunting prospect
A challenge to be faced, a test to be subject.

Yet even as the fear grips my heart
I cannot help but feel a thrill, a spark
For the time approaching is a time of growth
A time to shed the old and embrace the new.

So even as the shadows grow longer, still
I stand tall and steady, with a heart filled
With passion and determination, with hope and with fire
For the time approaching, I am ready and higher.

For I know that no matter what may come
I will face it head-on, with a heart on the run
Toward the future, toward the unknown
Toward the time approaching, to be fully grown.

Prisoner Within

Trapped within these walls of stone
A soul that longs to be alone
To break free from this prison within
To find peace, to find freedom from sin.

For every day is a battle, a fight
To keep hope alive, to keep the light
From fading away, from being snuffed out
By the darkness that surrounds and touts.

Its power and control, its hold on the soul
But I refuse to be its prisoner, to be its toll
I will fight and I will struggle; I will break free
From this prison within, this misery.

For I know that within me, there is a spark
A flame that burns bright that makes its mark
On the world around me, on those I hold dear
This flame, it is hope; it is my cheer

So even as I am held captive within
I will not let the darkness win
I will hold onto hope and onto love
And wait for the day when I am freed from above.

For I am more than a prisoner within
I am a soul that is strong and can begin
A new chapter, a new path, a new way
Out of this prison, into a brighter day.

Swansea, the Pretty Shitty City

Swansea pretty shitty city by the sea
A place of contrasts, both dark and free
A city of grime, a city of toil
A place that's often been called "spoil."

The streets are gritty; the air is thick
The factories loom, a constant tick
A city of industry, a city of trade
A place that's been shaped by its past.

The people here are a mix of the rough and the refined
A city of intelligence yet often maligned
For those who look beyond the surface dirt and grime
Will find a city of rich culture, a place of rhyme.

The docks are bustling; the ships come in
A constant reminder of the city's sin
For Swansea was built on the backs of its poor
A city that's been through so much more.

But the city is changing; it's on the rise
A new energy in its skies
Art and culture and a sense of pride
A city that's no longer satisfied.

With the status quo, it's moving forward
A city that's no longer ignored
For those who can see beyond the grime
Will find a city that's truly sublime.

Swansea a pretty shitty city by the sea
A place of contrasts, both dark and free
A city of grime, a city of toil
A place that's forever in turmoil.

But it's also a city of hope
A place where the future can cope
For Swansea is a city of resilience
A place that's never lost its brilliance.

I Love It the Way My Toes Curl When You Love Me

My toes curl, my body arches
As your love envelops me
A feeling of pure ecstasy
As you make love to me harder.

With every touch, every kiss
I am consumed by your bliss
A fiery passion, a burning desire
As you make love to me harder.

My mind races, my heart beats
As our bodies entwine
A symphony of pleasure and delight
As you make love to me harder.

Your hands explore, your lips claim
As you take me to new heights
A journey of pure ecstasy
As you make love to me harder.

With each thrust, each movement
I am yours, completely
A surrender of body and soul
As you make love to me harder.

Our bodies move in perfect rhythm
As we reach the peak of ecstasy
A moment of pure ecstasy
As you make love to me harder.

And as we lay, spent and sated
I am filled with love and gratitude
For the way you make love to me
Harder, deeper and with so much intensity.

So come, my love and make love to me harder
For in your arms, I am truly alive
And in this moment, I am yours, forever
As you make love to me harder.

Lost Thought

A thought once had now lost
A seed once planted, now tossed
Into the winds of time, to be forgotten
Or to be rediscovered, once more begotten.

But even as it is lost, it lingers on
In the corners of the mind, a faint dawn
Of an idea once had, a dream once dreamt
A spark that once ignited but now has been swept.

Into the shadows of memory, into the past
But the thought remains a seed that will last
For it is more than just a fleeting fancy
It is a seed of potential, of growth and of bounty.

So even as it may be lost, it is not gone
It is simply dormant, waiting to be reborn
To blossom into something new, something grand
A thought once lost, now found, now in hand.

For every thought, no matter how small
Has the power to inspire, to lift and to enthral
It is a spark of creativity, a flash of insight
A lost thought, waiting to be brought to light.

Lonely Donkey

A donkey stands alone in a field of grass
Its head held low; its spirit amass
With loneliness and sadness, with a heavy heart
It wanders aimlessly right from the start.

But even as it is lonely, it is not forsaken
For within it, there is a spark, a light unshaken
A hope that one day, its loneliness will end
And it will find its place, its purpose, its friend.

For every soul deserves to be loved and to belong
To have a home, a purpose, a song to sing
So even as the donkey stands alone, it must trust
That its loneliness will end and its hope will be just.

For one day, a kind soul will come its way
And bring it love and joy, a brighter day
The donkey will no longer feel alone
For it will have found its home, its own.

So, here's to the lonely donkey; may it find
The love and the joy it deserves and desires intertwined
May its loneliness fade and its hope ignite
May it find its place and its spirit take flight.

For every soul deserves to be loved and to belong
To have a home, a purpose, a song to sing
And The Lonely Donkey is no exception
May it find its way and its heart's inception.

Crazy Cat Lady

She is a woman like no other
A lover of felines, a true cat mother
She surrounds herself with a menagerie
Of fur babies, all purring with glee.

Her home is a haven, a feline paradise
Filled with love, warmth and cosy mice
For her, cats are her world, her everything
Her joy, her comfort, her soothing balm.

But to others, she may seem a bit mad
A crazy cat lady, a little bit sad
For they do not understand her love
For her fur babies, sent from above.

But she does not care, for she knows
That her love for her cats, it shows
In the way she cares for them, in the way she speaks
In the way she nurtures them, in the way she seeks.

To give them the best life, the best care
For they are her heart, her soul, her air
So, here's to the crazy cat lady; may she never change
May she continue to love and nurture, with love and with range.

Emotionally Exhausted

He is a young man with a heart full of pain
A soul that is weary, a spirit that is drained
By the weight of the world, by the weight of his emotions
By the loneliness that surrounds, like vast oceans.

He tries to hide it, to put on a brave face
But the exhaustion seeps through in every place
In the lines on his forehead, in the shadows under his eyes
In the way he moves, slow and with sighs.

He longs for connection, for love and for friendship
But his heart is guarded; his trust has been shipwrecked
By the wounds of the past, by the hurt and the pain
He finds it hard to open up, to let love remain.

But even as he is lonely, he is not alone
For within him, there is a spark, a light unknown
A hope that one day, he will find his way
Out of the darkness, into the day.

So, he keeps on going, even as it is hard
He holds onto hope like a lifeline, a guard
Against the loneliness, against the despair
He keeps on going, even as it wears.

For he knows that one day, he will find
The love and the happiness that is his intertwined
He will find his place, his purpose, his light
And his loneliness will fade into the night.

So, here's to the lonely young man; may he find
The love and the happiness he deserves and desires intertwined
May his loneliness fade and his heart open wide
To all the love and joy that the world has inside.

True Survivor

A true survivor is a force to be reckoned with
A spirit that refuses to be snuffed out, to be dismissed
They are warriors with hearts of steel
Unbreakable, unyielding, with a will to heal.

They have faced challenges that would break a lesser soul
But they have persevered and made themselves whole
They have climbed mountains and braved the storm
They have emerged victorious despite the odds.

They are not defined by their hardships and struggles
But by their resilience, their strength and their hustles
They are not victims but victors in their own right
They are survivors who have triumphed over the night.

They are a beacon of hope, a source of inspiration
They show us that no matter how dark the situation
There is always a way to overcome, to rise above
To be a survivor, a true survivor, with love.

So, here's to the true survivors; may they continue to shine
May they inspire us all to be strong and to find
The resilience within, to overcome and to thrive
For they are true survivors who have come alive.

A Lost Sibling

It's hard to lose a sibling and move on.
To accept that they're gone and carry on
But even in loss, there is hope and there is light
A way to honour them and make everything right.

For their memory lives on in all that we do
A guiding force that helps us to move through
The pain and the heartache of their absence here
A reminder to live and hold them dear.

So let their memory be a source of strength
A way to carry on and go to any length
To live our lives to the fullest extent
And make a difference in all that we've sent.

For they are with us in all that we do
A guiding light that helps us to see through
The darkness and the pain of their departure here
A reminder to love and to hold them dear.

So let their memory, be a beacon of hope
A way to carry on and find a way to cope
With the loss and the heartache that we've known
And let their memory inspire us to grow.

For even in loss, there is a way to find
A sense of purpose and a peace of mind
A way to honour them and all that they've done
And let their memory be a source of inspiration.

A Sudden Change of Wind

It comes without warning; a sudden gust
A shift in direction, an unexpected thrust
It changes the landscape; it changes the game
It shakes up the world and throws us into the same.

It brings with it uncertainty and a sense of unease
It disrupts the norm and leaves us to appease
The changes it brings, the challenges it poses
It tests our resilience, our adaptability and our composure.

But even as it may seem unsettling at first
It also brings with it new opportunities, a burst
Of fresh perspectives, of new beginnings
A chance to grow, to learn and to be winning.

So even as the wind may change its course
We must embrace the change and not let it force
Us into a corner, into a state of despair
We must embrace the change and let it prepare.

Us for the future, for what it may bring
We must be ready and let our hearts sing
With hope and with courage, with determination
For the sudden change of wind and its transformation.

Grieving Friend

I see the pain in your eyes, the sorrow in your heart
I feel the weight of your grief, tearing you apart
But know that you are not alone in this dark and lonely place
I am here with you to hold your hand, to see your face.

I may not have all the answers or know just what to say
But I am here to listen, to help in any way
I will hold you up when your strength is at an end
I will be your rock, your support, your friend.

For I know what it is to grieve, to feel lost and alone
To question the world and everything we've known
But I also know that with time and with love
The pain begins to ease and the light begins to shove.

Aside the darkness and bring in the day
It may not happen overnight, but it will come, I pray
So, hang on, my friend and take it one step at a time
And know that I am here to walk with you on this climb.

For even as you grieve, you are not alone
You have me and others, who care and who condone
Your feelings, your emotions, your pain and your fears
We are here for you through the joys and the tears.

So, let us help you to heal and to grow
To find your way, to find your light and to let it show
For you are a strong and amazing person, inside and out
And your grief does not define you, without a doubt.

So, take my hand and let's walk together
Through this journey, through this weather
Of grief and of healing, of love and of light
And know that I am here, with you, through the night.

Addiction

It starts with a choice, a moment of indulgence
But soon, it takes hold, with a fierce insistence
It consumes the mind; it controls the soul
It becomes a part of you, a dark and heavy toll.

It dictates your thoughts, your actions, your decisions
It becomes your master, your one true addiction
It takes away your freedom, your control
It leaves you feeling helpless, feeling alone.

But even as it takes, it also gives
A false sense of pleasure, a fleeting sense of bliss
It distracts you from reality, from the pain
It offers an escape, a temporary gain.

But it is an escape that is short-lived
An escape that comes at a high price that is misconstrued
For the more you indulge, the more you crave
The more it consumes until you are its slave.

And before you know it, it has taken everything
Your relationships, your dreams, your self-esteem
You are left with nothing but the addiction
A never-ending cycle, a constant affliction.

But it is never too late to break free
To take back control and to be
The person you were meant to be
To find the strength and the courage to see.

That you are more than the addiction
That you are worthy of love and affection
So, don't give up, don't lose hope
There is a way out, a way to cope.

With the addiction and all that it brings
There is a way to heal and to have wings
To fly above it all and find your way
To a life that is full, a life that is bright and colourful.

So, don't give up, my friend, don't give in
There is a way out, a way to begin
A new chapter, a new path, a new way
Away from the addiction and into the day.

So, hold onto hope and take it one step at a time
And know that you are not alone in this climb
For there are others who have been where you are
Who have found their way out, who have gone far.

In their journey of recovery and of healing
And they are here to support you and to be your shield
So, don't give up, my friend, keep on fighting
Keep on striving, keep on exciting.

The possibility of a life that is full and free
A life without addiction, a life just for thee
Hold onto hope and take it one day at a time
Seek support, seek guidance, seek to climb.

Out of the darkness and into the light
Away from the grip of addiction and into the fight
For you are strong, you are capable
You are worthy of love and you are lovable.

You are more than the addiction, more than the pain
You are a survivor and you will regain
Control of your life and your happiness
You will find your way and your peace and your blessedness.

So, don't give up, my friend, keep on going
Keep on striving, keep on growing
Into the person you were meant to be
A person of strength and courage and dignity.

So, don't give up and don't lose hope
There is a way out, a way to cope
With the addiction and all that it brings
There is a way to heal and to have wings
To fly above it all and find your way
To a life that is full, a life that is bright and colourful.

The Dark Night Ahead

The dark night looms, a shadow vast
A foreboding presence, a future cast
In shades of uncertainty, of fear and of doubt
It threatens to engulf and to shut out.

The light of hope, the light of love
It seems to smother and shove
Them aside, into the darkness and the cold
Leaving us to face the stories untold.

But even as the darkness seems to prevail
There is a spark, a light, a tale
Of resilience and strength, of courage and of might
A tale of hope that shines bright.

For even in the darkest of times
There is a way to find the light, the lines
Of hope and of healing, of love and of joy
A way to find our way and to employ.

The strength and the courage to face the night
To embrace the challenge and to fight
To find our way out and into the light
To find our way home and to ignite.

The spark within, the light within
To let it shine and let it begin
To guide us through the dark night ahead
To guide us home and to bed.

So even as the darkness seems to prevail
Hold onto hope and let it avail
To guide you through the challenges ahead
To guide you home and to bed.

A Deadly Kiss

A kiss that kills with poison sweet
Lips that taste like death, complete
A love that's doomed from the start
A beating heart that falls apart.

The venom courses through my veins
As I succumb to deadly pains
I thought I knew true love's embrace
But now I see I've made a mistake.

The darkness closes in; I fade away
My final thoughts of you, I can't convey
I should have known love's kiss could be
A deadly trap, as sweet as can be.

So beware, my love, of lips that burn
For a love like ours, there is no return
The kiss of death, it seems, is ours
Forever entwined in deadly powers.

Sexual Frustration

It gnaws at me, a constant ache
A fire that burns deep within
A need that I cannot forsake
But it is so often kept hidden.

It twists and turns, a tangled knot
A longing that I can't ignore
A desire that I cannot stop
But must be kept locked behind closed doors.

It is a feeling that I hate
But one that I cannot resist
A temptation that I must state
But it is something I cannot assist.

It is a feeling that is taboo
Something that I cannot express
A craving that is so true
But one that I must repress.

It is a feeling that I fear
For I know the damage it can bring
A lust that I must hold dear
But one that I must keep in check and cling.

So, I try to push it down
To keep it hidden and controlled
But it is a force that cannot be bound
A hunger that cannot be consoled.

And so, I live with this frustration
This longing that I cannot sate
A desire that causes agitation
But one that I must tolerate.

A Lust for Revenge

I burn with a fire deep within my soul
A desire for revenge that consumes me whole
I cannot rest until I see you pay
For the pain you've caused in such a cruel way.

I plot and I plan, in the dead of night
Dreaming of the moment when all will be right
When justice is served and you're left to rue
The day you crossed me and all that you do.

I am patient, but my patience has its limits
And when the time is right, I'll show you no mercy
I'll strike like a snake, swift and precise
Leaving you stranded with nowhere to hide.

You thought you were clever; you thought you were sly
But now you'll see just how wrong you can be
I'll be the one standing when all is said and done
You'll be the one begging for a second chance to run.

But it's too late for second chances now
My revenge will be sweet and I'll show you how
I'll watch as you fall from the heights you've reached
Leaving you broken and alone, bereft.

You thought you could play me for a fool
But now you'll see, I was playing you too
And when it's all over and the dust has cleared
You'll see that I won and you'll be left fearing
The day that you crossed me and all that you've done
For now, I have my revenge and it's time to move on.

The Four Elements of Life

The elements of life, they swirl and dance
Fire, earth, air and water, in a trance
Each one is unique and yet they all belong
Together, they create a beautiful song.

Fire, with its passion and its heat
Burning bright and hard to beat
Bringing light and warmth to everyday
A guiding force that shows us the way.

Earth, with its strength and its grounding force
A stable foundation for all that endures
Nourishing and sustaining, all that we see
A beautiful reminder of all we can be.

Air, with its breath and its gentle breeze
A whisper in our ear that never cease
Bringing new ideas and a fresh point of view
A vital element that keeps us feeling new.

Water, with its fluidity and its flow
A cleansing force that helps us to grow
Bringing life and renewal to everyday
A reminder to go with the flow and let it wash away.

The elements of life they come together
In a perfect balance, now and forever
Fire, earth, air and water, they combine
To create a world that is truly divine.

Accepting Defeat

It's hard to admit when we're in the wrong
To accept defeat and move on
To swallow our pride and let go of the fight
And admit that we lost without putting up a fight.

But sometimes, it's necessary to take a step back
To let go of our ego and let the past lack
To see the bigger picture and understand
That defeat is a part of life and it's not always bad.

For in defeat, we can find new strength
A renewed sense of purpose and a greater length
To reach for our goals and strive for the best
To learn from our mistakes and put them to the test.

So, let go of the anger and let go of the shame
And embrace the lessons that defeat can bring to the game
For it's through defeat that we can grow and evolve
And find a new path that we can truly solve.

So let go of the past and look to the future
With a new perspective and a renewed culture
For even in defeat, there is always a way
To rise up and conquer and make a new day
So, accept defeat and let it be a guide
To a better tomorrow and a more meaningful life.

A Corrupt Judge

The judge sits on the bench with a gavel in hand
A symbol of justice in this corrupt land
But justice is blind and this judge can't see
The harm and suffering that he causes to be.

For he is swayed by wealth and by power
He twists the law in his darkest hour
He ignores the truth and the facts of the case
And renders a verdict with no saving grace.

The defendants stand with their heads held low
As the judge pronounces their punishment, to show
He doesn't see the tears in their eyes
The broken families and the shattered lives.

For he is blinded by his own greed
He doesn't care about those in need
He only thinks of himself and his gain
Ignoring the harm that he causes to remain.

But justice will come in the end, they say
And this corrupt judge will have to pay
For all of the harm that he's caused over time
And the heartache and pain that he's left behind.

So let this be a lesson to all who would hear
That corruption has no place in the justice system here
And that one day, it will all come to light
And the corrupt judge will pay for his crimes with his life.

The Summertime Madness

Summertime madness is upon us again
The heat and the humidity it's a never-ending trend
We sweat and we pant and we fan ourselves silly
As we try to survive this summertime thrilly.

The ice cream is melting and so are we
We long for a breeze that will set us free
From the sticky and icky, the hot and the humid
But alas, it's summertime and we're stuck in it.

The pool is calling and so is the beach
We long for a dip in the cool and the sweet
But the sun is beating down and it's hard to escape
This summertime madness that's a big mistake.

We try to stay inside and turn on the AC
But it's no use, it's still hot and we're feeling quite lazy
We lay on the couch and we dream of the fall
When the weather is cooler and we can stand tall.

But until then, we'll just have to grin and bear it
This summertime madness that we can't share it
We'll drink lots of water and wear lots of sunscreen
And hope that this summer will come to an end soon.

So, let's embrace it and have some fun
This summertime madness that has just begun
We'll make the most of it and soak up the sun
And look forward to cooler days when the summer is done.

The King of Man

He stands tall and proud, with a noble heart
He is the King of Man and he'll never part
From the kingdom he loves and the people he serves
He is the shining light that the kingdom preserves.

He leads with honour and he always does right
He is the King of Man and he shines so bright
He is fair and just and he always does his best
To bring peace and prosperity to all of the rest.

He is a father to his people and his land
He is a protector of the peace that he has planned
He is a leader with a vision of the future
He is the King of Man and we are so grateful.

He is kind and compassionate to all those in need
He is the King of Man and he'll always lead
With a heart full of love and a mind full of grace
He is the shining example of a leader in this place.

He is always learning and he never stops growing
He is the King of Man and he's always knowing
What is best for his kingdom and his people, too
He is the leader we need to see us all through.

He is the King of Man and he'll always be there
To guide and to lead, with love and with care
He is the King of Man and he'll never let us down
He is the shining light that shines all around.

So, let's all raise a glass to the King of Man
The one who leads with honour and with a noble plan
The one who always does right and never stops trying
The one who is the King of Man and who is always shining.

The Two Rascals

Two naughty rascals, full of glee
They love to cause mischief, can't you see?
They run and they play all day long
Until the setting of the sun.

They climb and they jump, with all their might
They never stop, not for a single night
They are always on the go
Two little rascals, don't you know.

But even though they may cause some trouble
They bring so much joy to the double
They are full of life and love and fun
Two little rascals, second to none.

They may be little, but they have big hearts
Full of love and laughter right from the start
They bring joy to all those around
Their laughter a sweet and soothing sound.

No matter where they roam or play
They always find a way to brighten your day
Their energy is contagious; it's true
You can't help but smile when they come into view.

They may be mischievous, but they mean no harm
They are just two little rascals, full of charm
So let them run and let them play
For they bring happiness in their own special way.

Their curiosity knows no bounds
They are always eager to learn and be found
Two little rascals, full of life
Bringing joy to all, free from strife.

So let them be; let them roam free
For they are just being who they want to be
Two little rascals, full of cheer
Bringing joy to everyone, year after year.

The Storm in My Mind

The storm rages on, a force to be reckoned with
Its energy radiates a wild and frenzied pitch
The winds howl and the lightning cracks
As the rain pours down, a never-ending attack.

But within my mind, a spark is ignited
As the storm's energy is absorbed, my thoughts are ignited
Ideas flood my brain, a brainstorming frenzy
As I seek to find a way to help those around me.

The storm may rage on, its power unbridled
But I will not be swayed, my mind now filled
With determination and a fierce desire
To use this energy to fuel my fire.

I will not be deterred by the storm's fierce might
For its energy has given me new insight
I will use it to my advantage, a driving force
To help those in need, a noble source.

The storm may come and go, a fleeting presence
But its energy remains a potent essence
Fuelling my mind and inspiring change
As I strive to make a difference, to rearrange.

The world for the better, to bring hope and light
To those who may be lost in the storm's endless night
I will use this energy to guide my way
As I strive to make a brighter day.

So let the storm rage on; let it do its worst
For I have within me a burning thirst
To make a difference, to be a force for good
And with the energy of the storm, my goal is understood.

Player

He was a player through and through
A man who loved the game
He'd charm and flatter with words so smooth
Leaving hearts in flames.

He had no loyalty, no sense of right
He'd leave you in the dust
He'd take your love and hold it tight
Then toss it if he must.

He was a master of disguise
A snake with skin so sleek
He'd wrap you in his web of lies
And leave you feeling weak.

But oh, how sweet the taste of revenge
When his facade begins to fade
For, in the end, he'll meet his end
And his game of love will be played.

So beware, dear hearts, of this player's charms
For he will only bring you pain
Turn your back on him and all his harms
And seek love that is true and plain.

The Corrupt Mayor of My Town

The mayor, a man of power and might
A pillar of the community, or so they thought
But darkness lurked beneath his shining light
As secrets of his corruption were brought to court.

For years, he'd taken bribes and lied
His greed and lust for power knew no bounds
He'd trample on the weak and those who tried
To stop him, he'd simply run them down.

But now, his time has come to pay
As he stands trial before the law
His crimes and sins on full display
As justice works, to even the score.

The people watch with bated breath
As the verdict is handed down
They hope that he'll receive his death
And that a brighter future will be found.

But no matter what the outcome may be
This mayor's legacy is stained and cursed
He'll go down in history as a man who couldn't see
That corruption always ends in the worst.

So let this be a lesson to all who hold a seat
Of power and influence in this world
For, in the end, it's not what you achieve
But how you achieve it that matters most.

Identity

There was a young man, so full of life
Intelligence and wit, his heart rife
With the desire to be true to himself
But societal norms, they left him delved.

Into a world of confusion and doubt
His true identity, he couldn't figure out
He tried on different masks, hoping to find
A version of himself that would fit just fine.

But no matter how hard he tried, he couldn't shake
The feeling that something about him was fake
He felt like an impostor, living a lie
Wondering why he couldn't just be, simply, "I."

One day, he made a decision bold
To shed the skin of the person he was told
To be and embrace his true identity
It was a scary and uncertain journey, you see.

But as he embraced his true self, he found
A freedom and happiness, new and profound
He learned that it's okay to be different, to stand out
In a world that wants you to blend in and doubt.

So, here's to the young man, so brave and true
Who finally found his identity anew
May he live his life authentic and free
A sophisticated and interesting man, just like he always wanted to be.

Top Chef

His kitchen is a stage, a place to perform
Where ingredients are the instruments and his cooking the norm
He dances with the flames, a true maestro of the flame
Creating dishes that garner praise and acclaim.

His palate is refined, his taste discerning
His dishes are a reflection of his soul, unerring
He works tirelessly from dawn to dusk
To create culinary magic, it's his passion, a must.

This top chef's artistry is unmatched, it's clear to see
In each dish, a masterpiece for all the world to see
So, if you're in the mood for a dining experience, divine
Head on over to this top chef's restaurant; you'll be just fine.

A gourmet delight, from appetiser to dessert
This top chef's culinary skills will surely impart
A sense of satisfaction and pure joy
A dining experience, oh so coy
So come and dine and taste the art
Of this top chef, a culinary master at heart.

Top Boss

Top Boss, leader of the land
A guiding hand, a master plan
With vision clear and strategy, sound
Your team is bound to be renowned.

You inspire us to aim for the stars
To reach for goals beyond what seems far
You show us how to work and play
To give our all each and every day.

Your words of wisdom ring true
They lead us to a brighter hue
You are the one we look up to
Top Boss, we are grateful for you.

Your guidance helps us grow and thrive
You show us how to truly strive
For excellence in all we do
Top Boss, we are grateful to.

You lead with grace and poise
Your decisions are always wise
You are the one we trust and respect
Top Boss, you are the best.

With you at the helm, we can't go wrong
Your leadership keeps our spirits strong
We are proud to be a part of your team
Top Boss, you are the cream of the cream.

So, here's to you, our Top Boss
We raise a glass, no matter the cost
Thank you for all that you do
Top Boss, we are grateful to you.

Miracle in My Bed, 2022

Kamil Aleksander Kempczyński, a faithful Latter-Day Saint
Sat in meditation, deep in contemplation
He pondered the lives of Adam and Eve
And through his belief in Jesus, he did believe.

He realised they had not been baptised
And through his faith, he offered it with utmost pride
As he lay in bed, on either side, he saw
Adam and Eve ascend to heaven, hand in hand, with awe.

The miracle that occurred was pure and divine
As Kamil's faith and belief, did truly shine
In that moment, he knew the power of prayer
And how the Lord, does truly care.

With open hearts, Adam and Eve
Accepted the baptism and were set free
Their journey to heaven was a sight to see
As Kamil's faith brought them to eternity.

This miracle, a testament to the Lord's might
And how, through faith and belief, our souls take flight
Kamil's experience a reminder to all
That with Jesus, we shall never fall.

So let us meditate and ponder with care
The lives of our ancestors and the path we must bear
For through belief in Jesus, we too shall ascend
And with Him, our eternal happiness shall never end.

Never-Ending Disaster

It starts with a rumble, a shake of the ground
A warning of what is yet to come
A never-ending disaster, a force to be reckoned with
Leaving destruction and chaos in its wake, undone.

The skies turn dark, the winds whip and howl
Tearing down homes, upending lives
Families flee, seeking shelter and safety
As the disaster rages on, no end in sight.

The aftermath is a scene of devastation
Rubble and debris, as far as the eye can see
Broken lives and shattered dreams
The toll of the disaster, a tragedy.

But in the midst of the chaos and loss
There is hope, there is light
People come together, lend a helping hand
In the face of the never-ending disaster, unite.

They work to rebuild, to restore
To bring life back to the place they call home
They find strength in each other
In the face of the never-ending disaster, roam.

For even in the darkest of times
When it feels like all is lost
There is always a way forward
A path to a brighter future, no matter the cost.

So let us stand tall; let us persevere
In the face of the never-ending disaster
For though it may seem overwhelming
We are stronger than we could ever imagine.

The Never-Ending Urge

The never-ending urge it gnaws at my soul
A constant craving, a constant goal
It whispers to me, a seductive voice
Promising satisfaction, a moment of rejoice.

It consumes me, a flame that never dies
A hunger that grows no matter how I try
To ignore it, to push it aside
It always returns, a relentless tide.

I try to resist, to turn away
But it lures me back, day after day
It's a craving I can't seem to shake
An obsession I can't seem to break.

I know I should let it go, let it fade
But it's a part of me, a part that's engraved
A need that runs deep, a desire that burns
An urge that I can't seem to spurn.

So, I give in, succumb to the call
And in that moment, I lost it all
The control I thought I had, the strength I thought I knew
It all slips away, a fleeting dew.

But even as I fall, the urge remains
A constant presence, a constant pain
It tugs at me, a puppet on a string
And I know that this cycle it will never end.

So, I try to find balance, to find my way
To let the urge have its say
But to keep it in check, to keep it in bounds
To keep it from consuming me, consuming all that surrounds.

The never-ending urge, it's a part of me
And though it may drive me to my knees
I'll keep on fighting, keep on striving
To keep it in check, to keep on thriving.

Life Is Full of Compromises

Life is full of compromises, a constant give-and-take
We make choices every day, decisions we must make
We weigh the pros and cons; we try to do what's right
But sometimes, it's hard to see the path in sight.

We try to find our way, to find our place in the world
But sometimes it seems like we're just a tiny cog, whirled
In the great machine of life, lost in the fray
Searching for meaning, searching for our way.

We make sacrifices; we give up things we love
In the hope of something more, a brighter future above
We choose the road less travelled or the one well-worn
Hoping it will lead us to where we want to be, forlorn.

But life is unpredictable, a fickle friend at best
It twists and turns and upsets all the rest
Of our plans and our dreams and we're left to adopt
To the changes that come and to the hand we're dealt.

We try to be strong to weather the storm
But sometimes it's hard and we feel so worn
We wonder why we bother, why we even try
But somehow, we find the strength and we keep on with life.

So, we compromise, we make the best of what we have
We find a way to make it work, to find a path
That leads us forward and we keep on going
We may not know where we're going, but we keep on rowing.

We may not have it all, but we have each other
And that's enough, that's all we need to weather
The storms of life and to find our way
Through all the ups and downs and all the twists and turns we face.

So, when life gets tough and you feel like you're stuck
Just remember that you're not alone and that you're luckier than most
There are people who love you, who will help you through
And together, you'll find a way to make it through.

The Saddest of Thoughts

The saddest of thoughts, it came to me
Like a bolt out of the blue, suddenly
It struck me down and left me bereft
My spirit devastated, my heart left cleft.

It was a thought I never wanted to face
A truth I never wanted to embrace
But it was there, staring me in the eye
A thought that made me want to die.

I tried to push it away, to run and hide
But it followed me, a shadow at my side
It taunted me, a constant refrain
A voice that whispered my deepest pain.

I couldn't escape it, no matter how I tried
It was a part of me, forever inside
A weight that I could never shed
A thought that left me feeling dead.

But even as I lay there, broken and alone
I knew that I had to find my way back home
To the land of the living, to the light of day
I had to find a way to make it okay.

So, I gathered my strength and I stood up tall
And I faced the thought and I let it fall
I let it go and I left it behind
And though it still haunts me, I don't let it bind.

Me to the past or to the pain
I let it be and I choose to gain
The strength to move on, to find my way
To live my life each and every day.

The saddest of thoughts, it came and it went
But it didn't break me, it didn't dent
My spirit or my will to survive
I faced it down and I'm still alive.

The State of Shock

The state of shock it hits you like a wave
A sudden onset, a sudden grave
Feeling of loss, a feeling of dread
Your mind is numb; your heart feels dead.

You try to process, to make sense of it all
But the thoughts won't come; you feel so small
Like a tiny speck in an endless sea
Drifting aimlessly, lost and aimlessly.

You try to react, to do what needs to be done
But your body won't move, your mind won't run
It's like you're stuck in a never-ending loop
A prisoner of your own mind, in a prison that's not so crude.

You feel disconnected from the world around
Like you're watching it all from a place that's profound
But not a part of it, not truly there
A ghost haunting the living, a shadow unaware.

The state of shock, it's a cruel and heartless beast
It eats away at you leaves you at least
A shell of your former self, a shadow of your soul
Leaving you lost and alone in a black and endless hole.

But even in the darkest of days, the light can still shine
And somehow, through the fog, you'll find a way to shine
A way to heal, a way to move on
To find your way back home to where you belong.

So, don't give up, don't give in
You're stronger than you think; don't let the shock win
Find your feet, find your voice
And you'll find your way and you'll have a choice.

To live your life, to be who you are
To heal and to grow, to reach for the stars
The state of shock, it's a temporary thing
You'll find your way through it and you'll start to sing.

Disco in the Graveyard

In the graveyard, where the dead do lay
A Disco beat begins to play
The spirits rise from the graves
To groove and dance on hallowed pave.

Their bones a-clacking', in a skeletal sway
Ghostly figures boogie the night away
The moon is full; the stars shine bright
It's a Disco party in the graveyard tonight.

With ectoplasmic flares and misty beams
The ghouls and ghosts perform disco-inspired themes
Skeletons in bell bottoms and zombies in Afros
Get down to the beat, with no need for a pose.

The headstones act as the DJ booth
As the dead let loose, with their spooky booth
A grave-yard smash, a howling hit
The undead are having a Disco graveyard fit.

The mummy unwraps to reveal a grin
And the werewolf howls as the party begin
The vampires they sparkle in the Disco light
While the zombies, they dance with all their might.

The end of the night is drawing near
But the party isn't over; there's no need to fear
As the living, they leave with a spooky thrill
The Disco graveyard party will go on still.

So, if you hear a beat, in the graveyard's still
Don't be afraid, just let your feet fill
With the rhythm of the night and let it guide
To the Disco graveyard, where the dead reside.

Another Love

Another love, oh, what a thrill
A new romance, a chance to fill
The emptiness left by the past
A love that's sure to make love last.

But wait, what's this I see and hear
A familiar face, a voice so dear
My heart is torn, my mind confused
This new love's standing right beside my muse.

What's a man to do in this fix
A heart that's torn, a mind that's mixed
I'll tell you what I'll do, my friend
I'll love them both until the very end.

For two is better than one, you see
Two hearts that beat as one in harmony
One for the day, one for the night
One for the laughter, one for the fight.

One for the love that's sweet and pure
One for the love that's wild and obscure
Two sides to every coin, you know
And I'll take them both, don't you know.

But shh, don't tell a soul, my dears
Our little secret will stay right here
For love is love and that's all that matters
And in love, two's always better than one, that's what it matters.

So come and join me in this dance
Of love and laughter and second chance
For in the end, we'll all see
Two's always better than one, you and me.

Used up Tears

Used-up tears dried upon my face
A reminder of my love's disgrace
But wait, what's this? A smile I spy
For tears are but a part of life, oh my.

Used-up tears, a thing of the past
A chapter closed; a new love forecast
For every tear that falls from my eye
A new opportunity for love doth lie.

Used-up tears, a sign of growth
A reminder that love is a game we play, so bold
And every heartbreak, every cry
Is but a stepping stone to love that's nigh.

Used up tears, a badge of honour
A testament to my heart's valour
For every tear, a lesson learned
And love, in turn, my heart has earned.

Used up tears, a work of art
A tapestry woven with a lover's heart
For every tear, a thread is spun
And love, the fabric of our lives, is done.

Used up tears, a part of love's lore
A reminder that love is worth fighting for
So let your tears flow, my dear
For love, in all its forms, is always near.

Used-up tears, a thing of beauty
A reminder that love is the ultimate duty
So, dry your eyes and take a stand
For love is the gift that keeps on giving, you understand.

So, let's raise a glass to love, my friends
And to the tears that love attends
For every tear that falls from our eyes
Is but a sign that love still thrives.

Catching Shadows

Catching Shadows, a dangerous game
In the darkness, our hearts aflame
A hunt for what lurks in the night
Our souls on the edge, ready for a fight.

We roam the streets with eyes aglow
In search of the unknown, to catch and know
The shadows that linger in the corners deep
Our souls they keep while they creep and creep.

But be warned, dear hunters, as you set out
These shadows they are not what they're about
A monster, a ghoul, a being of fear
Will consume your soul if you come too near.

So, arm yourself with knowledge and wit
For in the shadows, danger doth sit
And as you hunt, with caution and care
Remember that some shadows are not to be ensnared.

For in the darkness lurks a different kind
The shadows that feed on the weak of mind
They devour your soul, your will, your might
Leaving you nothing but eternal night.

So be careful, dear hunters, as you search and seek
For the shadows, they are not all meek
There are those that bring death and misery
And once caught, there's no release, no sanctuary.

So, think twice, dear hunters, before you start
For catching shadows, can tear you apart
The darkness is deep and the shadows are vast
And once caught, there's no going back; it is cast.

So, take heed, dear hunters, as you roam
For the shadows are not always ones to be known
For those who dare to play this game
Will find that the shadows are not the same.

Movie Fanatic

Movie fanatic, oh so keen
Your love for films is quite serene
From drama to comedy, you've seen it all
Your movie collection an impressive haul.

Your home is filled with posters galore
From classic films to ones before your time
Your Blu-ray shelf is an endless floor
Of stories waiting to unwind.

You've memorised every line and scene
From *Casablanca* to *The Queen*
You know the actors and their works
From early roles to their quirks.

You've sat through endless marathons
To see your favourites, one by one
You've even dressed up as your favourite lead
Your love for film, you're not afraid to plead.

You'll never turn down a trip to the cinema
You'll always be the first in line to see the new releases
Your love for film will never dissipate
It's a love affair and it's simply great.

So, here's to you, dear movie fanatic
May your love for film be ever manic
May you always have a film to watch
And a theatre seat, front row, notched.

Your love for film is truly grand
A love that will forever stand
So, keep on watching oh movie buff
Your love for film, it's simply enough.

A Poetic Observer

A mind attuned to beauty and grace
A heart that beats in perfect time
A soul that seeks to find its place
In the vast and complex design.

This poetic observer stands apart
From the chaos of the world
A beacon in the darkest part
A banner unfurled.

With eyes that see beyond the veil
And ears that hear the silent song
This observer will not fail
To right the wrong.

For in each word, each thought, each line
Lies the power to inspire
To lift the spirit, to refine
And set the soul on fire.

So let us all be poetic observers
Seekers of truth and beauty's call
For in this role, no one proffers
A more noble role of all.

Trail of Broken Hearts

He wandered through the land
Leaving broken hearts behind
A trail of tears and shattered dreams
That stretched on for miles and miles.

He never meant to cause such pain
But somehow, it always seemed
That wherever he went, hearts were lain
Bare and raw, exposed and gleamed.

He told himself it wasn't his fault
That love was fleeting and hard to hold
But deep inside, a voice was assaulting
A truth that couldn't be controlled.

For he knew that he was the cause
Of all the heartache and the woe
That he was the one who paused
At the threshold of love's great flow.

He tried to change, to turn his back
On the life he'd led before
But the heartbreak trail was a hard track
To walk alone and never more.

So, he wandered on, a troubled soul
Searching for a way to right his wrongs
Hoping to find a heart made whole
And leave the heartbreak trail behind.

But the trail he left will never fade
A scar upon the hearts he left behind
A reminder of the love that once played
But in the end, it could not be intertwined.

The Meaning of Life

Of life's meaning, we may never know
For it is a mystery, deep and profound
Some say it's love that helps us grow
While others claim it can be found.

In the pursuit of wealth and fame
Or the search for truth and enlightenment
Yet still, others say it's just a game
And life has no real significance.

But perhaps the meaning of life lies
In the simple things that bring us joy
The laughter of a child, the warmth of the sun
The love of family and friends, a beautiful sunset, a well-cooked meal.

So perhaps the meaning of life is not a grand design
But the sum of all the moments that make us feel alive
The moments that bring us purpose and delight
And fill our hearts with love and light.

I Believe

In the vast expanse of existence, I am the architect of my destiny, forging a symphony of purpose with each step I take.

I am the master of my thoughts, weaving a tapestry of positivity that resonates through the corridors of my mind, unlocking the boundless potential within.

In the crucible of challenges, I am the alchemist transmuting adversity into opportunity, harnessing the transformative power of every experience.

I am the embodiment of resilience, standing tall amidst the tempests of life, my roots anchored in the fertile soil of self-belief.

Through the labyrinth of uncertainty, I am the compass guiding me towards the true north of my aspirations, fuelled by an unwavering commitment to my dreams.

I am the curator of my emotions, sculpting them into tools of strength and compassion, fostering connections that radiate with empathy.

As I navigate the celestial dance of time, I am the maestro conducting the orchestra of my moments, savouring the cadence of each breath with mindful awareness.

I am the seeker of knowledge, embracing the continuous evolution of my understanding, a perpetual student in the grand university of life.

In the realm of possibilities, I am the trailblazer carving paths untrodden, igniting the flames of innovation that illuminate the darkness of the unknown.

I am the beacon of self-love, radiating a luminous aura that nurtures my spirit, casting away the shadows of doubt that may attempt to linger.

Through the ebb and flow of existence, I am the river of gratitude, recognizing the abundance that flows into my life and cascading it back with heartfelt appreciation.

I am the embodiment of empowerment, a force that harmonizes with the universe, resonating with the cosmic vibrations that propel me towards my highest potential.

In the mirror of self-reflection, I am the mirror itself, gazing into the depths of my soul, acknowledging the beauty that lies within, and embracing the imperfections that add character to my being.

As I tread the intricate mosaic of relationships, I am the compassionate gardener, nurturing connections with tenderness, cultivating a garden where love and understanding bloom perennially.

I am the sentinel of boundaries, recognizing the sacred space within, guarding against energies that seek to diminish my inner light.

In the theatre of action, I am the protagonist of my narrative, crafting a story of purpose and impact, leaving an indelible mark on the stage of existence.

With every heartbeat, I am the rhythm of vitality coursing through my veins, an echo of life's pulsating energy reverberating within the chambers of my heart.

I am the embodiment of courage, facing the shadows of fear with unwavering valour, transcending limitations to unveil the boundless horizon of my capabilities.

In the kaleidoscope of perspectives, I am the prism refracting understanding, appreciating the diversity of thought that enriches the mosaic of collective wisdom.

I am the weaver of dreams, threading the fabric of my aspirations with determination, creating a tapestry that unfolds into the masterpiece of my fulfilled destiny.

As I traverse the crossroads of decision, I am the navigator guided by intuition, trusting the compass of my inner knowing to lead me towards the paths aligned with my soul's purpose.

In the embrace of solitude, I am the companion to my own soul, finding solace in the silence, and discovering the profound wisdom that resides in the stillness.

I am the emissary of kindness, sowing seeds of benevolence wherever I tread, nurturing a garden of goodwill that blossoms in the hearts of those I encounter.

In the dance of collaboration, I am the harmonious partner, contributing my unique melody to the symphony of shared endeavours, co-creating a masterpiece of collective achievement.

I am the alight spirit, soaring on the wings of authenticity, embracing my true essence with grace, and radiating a luminosity that inspires others to illuminate their own paths.

In the mosaic of setbacks, I am the phoenix rising from the ashes of challenges, reborn with newfound strength and resilience, transcending obstacles as stepping stones towards greater heights.

I am the guardian of balance, attuned to the equilibrium of mind, body, and spirit, cultivating a holistic well-being that fuels my journey with vitality.

In the cosmic dance of interconnectedness, I am the thread weaving through the fabric of humanity, recognizing the oneness that unites us all in the tapestry of existence.

I am the embodiment of gratitude, a beacon of appreciation that illuminates the blessings scattered along my life's journey, fostering a perpetual state of abundance.

In the silence of contemplation, I am the sage absorbing the profound lessons whispered by the universe, integrating the wisdom that emanates from the cosmic whispers.

I am the seeker of enlightenment, delving into the depths of consciousness, unravelling the mysteries of existence, and aligning my soul with the universal truths that guide my path.

I am the torchbearer of legacy, imprinting the sands of time with the footprints of purpose, leaving a trail for generations to follow in the pursuit of their own destinies.

As I stand at the crossroads of destiny, I am the architect of my fate, wielding the chisel of intention to carve a sculpture of purpose that stands as a testament to the legacy I leave behind.

In the grand symphony of life, I am the maestro of my destiny, orchestrating a composition of empowerment, resilience, and boundless love that reverberates through the corridors of eternity.

January

The first month of the year a time to reflect
On the memories and moments, we've left
In the past, a time to embrace
New beginnings, a time to face.

The challenges ahead, to let our spirits rise
With determination in our eyes
We set our goals and chase our dreams
With the hope that anything is possible, or so it seems.

In January, the weather is cold and crisp
The days are short, the nights are brisk
But that doesn't stop us from moving forward
From striving towards a brighter future.

We bundle up in coats and gloves
To brave the snow and icy slush
We embrace the winter, we don't hide
We face it head-on, with strength and pride.

In January, we celebrate the New Year
With fireworks and confetti, without fear
We look back on the past and all that we've done
And look ahead to the future with hope and fun.

We make resolutions, we set our sights
On the things we want to achieve and the goals we want to ignite
We vow to be better, to be kind and true
To follow our hearts and do what we must do.

So, let's embrace the month of January
With open arms and hearts that are merry
Let's make the most of every day
And let our spirits shine and play.

Here's to a new beginning, a fresh start
To a year full of hope, love and heart
Happy January may it be bright
Filled with joy and love, with all our might.

February

The second month of the year a time to heal
From the heartaches and wounds that we feel
A time to move forward, to let go
Of the past and all its woe.

February is a month of love and cheer
A time to celebrate those we hold dear
From Valentine's Day to President's Day
There's always a reason to brighten our way.

In February, the weather is cold and grey
But that doesn't stop us from finding our way
To the warmth of love and friendship's glow
To chase away the winter's cold.

We bundle up in scarves and hats
To brave the snow and icy flats
We embrace the winter; we don't run
We face it head-on, with fun and pun.

In February, we honour the past
We remember those who came before us at last
We pay tribute to their lives and deeds
And all the memories that we keep.

We make plans for the future; we set our sights
On the things we want to achieve and the goals we want to ignite
We vow to be better, to be kind and true
To follow our hearts and do what we must do.

So, let's embrace the month of February
With open arms and hearts that are merry
Let's make the most of every day
And let our spirits shine and play.

Here's to a month of love and light
To a February that's warm and bright
Happy February, may it be sweet
Filled with love and joy, with all our heat.

March

The third month of the year a time to emerge
From the winter's grasp, to let our spirit's surge
With energy and excitement, to embrace
The spring and all its grace.

March is a month of renewal and growth
A time to let our spirit's overflow
With the possibility of a new season
A time to chase our dreams and reason.

In March, the weather is still cold at night
But the days are getting longer, the light
It is brighter, the air is warmer and mild
A hint of spring, a welcome child.

We shed our coats and gloves; we feel alive
As the world awakens, we thrive
We embrace the change, we don't fear
We welcome the spring, it's very clear.

In March, we honour the past
We remember those who came before us at last
We pay tribute to their lives and deeds
And all the memories that we keep.

We make plans for the future; we set our sights
On the things we want to achieve and the goals we want to
ignite
We vow to be better, to be kind and true
To follow our hearts and do what we must do.

So, let's embrace the month of March
With open arms and hearts that are starch
Let's make the most of every day
And let our spirits shine and play.

Here's to a month of new beginnings
Of chasing our dreams and winning
Here's to a month of hope and love
To a bright and shining March above.

April

In April's tender grasp, a tapestry unfolds
A canvas of rebirth, where stories are told
Whispers of raindrops on windowsills play
As nature dons a gown of blossoms in array.

The air, a symphony or fragrant allure
Petrichor lingers, an essence so pure
A ballet of petals in delicate hues
Nature's choreography, the stage she woos.

Amidst the canvas of burgeoning green
April's caress, a magical scene
The sun, a painter with a golden brush
Illuminates the world, a verdant hush.

Each dew-kissed morning, a whispered hymn
A sonnet of beginnings, a promise within
The breeze, a poet, stirs the burgeoning leaves
Verse upon verse, as nature conceives.

In April's embrace, where dreams softly tread
Life unfurls, an awakening spread
A dance with time, as seconds unfurl
April, a chapter in nature's vast swirl.

A serenade of birds in the early dawn
April's awakening, a rebirth drawn
With every bud and bloom in tender grace
April whispers tales of a sublime chase.

In this nuanced verse, where beauty resides
April, the poet, in eloquence abides
A month in stanzas, nature's lyrical skill
April's embrace, an eternal thrill.

May

In May's embrace, a tapestry refined
Nature's artistry, a masterpiece designed
Petals unfurl in a ballet of grace
As spring's enchantment paints the space.

The sun ascends with a golden kiss
Illuminating landscapes in sweet bliss
Leaves rustle in a soft, poetic rhyme
May's arrival, an ephemeral paradigm.

Blossoms burst forth in fragrant hues
A chorus of life, a vibrant muse
Nature's symphony, a melody profound
May, the maestro, orchestrates around.

Gentle zephyrs weave through the air
Caressing blooms with a tender care
In May's tableau, a verdant scene
Life awakens in hues serene.

Each dawn a verse, a lyrical note
In May's embrace, dreams devote
A canvas painted with strokes divine
Nature's opus, in May's design.

With every day, a new chapter unfolds
May's narrative, a story retold
In this sonnet spun by nature's hand
May graces the earth, a poetic strand.

June

The sixth month of the year a time to shine
To let our spirits burst forth, to intertwine
With the warmth and light of the summer sun
As the days grow longer, the fun.

Begins a time for growth and play
To let our spirits roam and stray
From the routine and monotony
To embrace the world, to be free.

In June, the weather is hot and bright
The days are longer, the nights are light
The air is fragrant with the scent of flowers
Nature awakens; it's a shower.

Of beauty and colour, a sight to behold
As the world comes alive, young and old
We shed our coats and gloves; we feel alive
As the world awakens, we thrive.

In June, we honour the past
We remember those who came before us at last
We pay tribute to their lives and deeds
And all the memories that we keep.

We make plans for the future; we set our sights
On the things we want to achieve and the goals we want to
ignite
We vow to be better, to be kind and true.

To follow our hearts and do what we must do
So, let's embrace the month of June
With open arms and hearts that are fine
Let's make the most of every day.

And let our spirits shine and play
Here's to a month of growth and renewal
To a June that's full of fun and all that is cool
May it bring joy and love to your heart.

And may it be a month that sets the start
Of a summer filled with endless delight
May June be a time for your spirits to take flight.

July

July, oh July, the month of summer's peak
The air is hot; the sun burns bright
The days are long, the nights short and sweet
Nature's canvas painted in shades of gold and heat.

The grass is dry; the trees are green
The cicadas sing their deafening song
The water sparkles in the afternoon sun
A shimmering pool of liquid fun.

The fruit is ripe, the vegetables are plump
The farmers work from dawn till dusk
Harvesting the bounty of the land
A feast to share with family and friends.

Children laugh and play outside
No school to keep them confined
Swimming and running, free as can be
July is the month of pure joy and glee.

But as the days turn into nights
The fireflies emerge, tiny specks of light
Twinkling and flickering, a magical sight
Until they fade away into the morning light.

July, oh July, the month of fire
A time for heat, a time for desire
Embrace the warmth, embrace the light
For July is a gift from the sun's bright might.

So let us soak up every ray
Of summer's warmth on this longest day
Let us dance and sing and laugh and play
For July is here and it's time to sway.

August

August, oh August, the last month of summer's reign.
The days grow shorter, the nights grow longer
Nature's canvas painted in shades of gold and amber
As the leaves begin to turn, a symphony of colour.

The air is hot; the sun still burns bright
But a hint of coolness dances on the night
The fruit is ripe, the vegetables are plump
The farmers work from dawn till dusk.

Children laugh and play outside
But the end of summer is nowhere in sight
They swim and run free as can be
August is the month of pure joy and glee.

But as the days turn into nights
The fireflies emerge, tiny specks of light
Twinkling and flickering, a magical sight
Until they fade away into the morning light.

August, oh August, the month of change
A time for growth, a time for rearranging
Embrace the warmth, embrace the light
For August is a gift, a final summer's sight.

So let us soak up every ray
Of summer's warmth on this longest day
Let us dance and sing and laugh and play
For August is here and it's time to sway.

But as the month draws to a close
We must say goodbye to summer's prose
We must bid farewell to the sun's bright light
And embrace the cooler days of fall's might.

August, oh August, the end is near
But the memories will last all year
So let us make the most of every day
And cherish the warmth while it stays.

September

September, the ninth month of the year
The air is cool, the leaves rearrange
Nature's canvas painted in shades of red and gold
As the trees prepare for winter's cold.

The days grow shorter, the nights grow longer
But the sun still shines, a beacon of warmth
The fruit is ripe, the vegetables are plump
The farmers work from dawn till dusk.

Children return to school, their summer fun at an end
But the memories will last, a never-ending trend
They learn and grow, their minds alight
September is the month of new beginnings and insight.

But as the days turn into nights
The fireflies are gone, their magic out of sight
The stars come out, twinkling and bright
Until the dawn breaks and the day takes flight.

September, the month of balance
A time for work, a time for abundance
Embrace the cool, embrace the light
For September is a gift, a time to make things right.

So, let us embrace the changing season
And all the joys and treasures it will bring
Let us make the most of every day
And welcome the cooler weather's sway.

For even as summer fades away
There is still much beauty to be displayed
In the red and gold of the falling leaves
And the warm and cosy days that September weaves.

October

October, the month of pumpkin spice and falling leaves
A time of change, a time for new beginnings and new beliefs
Nature's canvas painted in shades of red and gold
As the trees prepare for winter's cold.

The days grow shorter, the nights grow longer
But the sun still shines, a beacon of warmth
The fruit is ripe, the vegetables are plump
The farmers work from dawn till dusk.

Children continue to learn and grow
Their minds expanding, their spirits aglow
They play and laugh, their hearts alight
October is the month of pure delight.

But as the days turn into nights
The fireflies are gone, their magic out of sight
The stars come out, twinkling and bright
Until the dawn breaks and the day takes flight.

October, the month of Halloween
A time for costumes, a time for screams
A time for tricks, a time for treats
A time to let your inner monster meets.

October, the month of change
A time for growth, a time to rearrange
Embrace the cool, embrace the light
For October is a gift, a time to make things right.

So, let us embrace the changing season
And all the joys and treasures it will bring
Let us make the most of every day
And welcome the cooler weather's sway.

October's beauty is on display
In the colours of the leaves, in the warmth of the day
It's a month of change, a time to prepare
For the cooler months ahead, but with love and care.

November

November, the month of crisp air and falling leaves
A time of change, a time for rest and ease
Nature's canvas painted in shades of brown and gold
As the trees shed their leaves, a story untold.

The days grow shorter, the nights grow longer
But the sun still shines, a beacon of warmth
The fruit is gone, the vegetables are few
The farmers rest; their work is through.

Children continue to learn and grow
Their minds expanding, their spirits aglow
They play and laugh, their hearts alight
November is the month of pure delight.

But as the days turn into nights
The fireflies are gone, their magic out of sight
The stars come out, twinkling and bright
Until the dawn breaks and the day takes flight.

November, the month of Thanksgiving
A time for family, a time for giving thanks
A time for feasts, a time for love
A time to be grateful for the blessings from above.

November, the month of change
A time for rest, a time to rearrange
Embrace the cool, embrace the light
For November is a gift, a time to make things right.

So, let us embrace the changing season
And all the joys and treasures it will bring
Let us make the most of every day
And welcome the cooler weather's sway.

November's beauty is on display
In the colours of the leaves, in the warmth of the day
It's a month of gratitude, a time to give thanks
For the blessings in our lives and the love that we have.

December

December, the month of holiday cheer
A time for family, a time for good cheer
Nature's canvas painted in shades of white and cold
As the world prepares for winter's hold.

The days grow shorter, the nights grow longer
But the sun still shines, a beacon of warmth
The fruit is gone, the vegetables are few
The farmers rest; their work is through.

Children continue to learn and grow
Their minds expanding, their spirits aglow
They play and laugh, their hearts alight
December is the month of pure delight.

But as the days turn into nights
The fireflies are gone, their magic out of sight
The stars come out, twinkling and bright
Until the dawn breaks and the day takes flight.

December, the month of Christmas
A time for gifts, a time for wishes
A time for love, a time for joy
A time to come together for girls and boys.

December, the month of Hanukkah
A time for candles, a time for latkes
A time for family, a time for love
A time to celebrate, to push and shove.

December, the month of change
A time for rest, a time to rearrange
Embrace the cool, embrace the light
For December is a gift, a time to make things right.

So, let us embrace the changing season
And all the joys and treasures it will bring
Let us make the most of every day
And welcome the colder weather's sway.

For even as autumn fades away
There is still much beauty to be displayed
In the white and cold of the falling snow
And the warm and cosy days that December knows.